Photography: Glen S. Axelrod, Mary Bloom, courtesy of Fabulous Ferrets, Isabelle Francais, Michael Gilroy, Gary Kaskel, Dr. Michael Leach, Dr. Damon Miller, Mervin F. Roberts, Linda Smothers, Wendy Winsted. **Drawings:** John R. Quinn.

Dedication

This book is dedicated to Dr. Emil Dolensek, Chief Veterinarian for the New York Zoological Society (The Bronx Zoo).

1995 Edition

9 8 7 6 5 4 3 2 1   9 5 6 7 8 9

Distributed in the UNITED STATES to the Pet Trade by T.F.H. Publications, Inc., One T.F.H. Plaza, Neptune City, NJ 07753; distributed in the UNITED STATES to the Bookstore and Library Trade by National Book Network, Inc. 4720 Boston Way, Lanham MD 20706; in CANADA to the Pet Trade by H & L Pet Supplies Inc., 27 Kingston Crescent, Kitchener, Ontario N2B 2T6; Rolf C. Hagen Ltd., 3225 Sartelon Street, Montreal 382 Quebec; in CANADA to the Book Trade by Vanwell Publishing Ltd., 1 Northrup Crescent, St. Catharines, Ontario L2M 6P5 ; in ENGLAND by T.F.H. Publications, PO Box 15, Waterlooville PO7 6BQ; in AUSTRALIA AND THE SOUTH PACIFIC by T.F.H. (Australia), Pty. Ltd., Box 149, Brookvale 2100 N.S.W., Australia; in NEW ZEALAND by Brooklands Aquarium Ltd. 5 McGiven Drive, New Plymouth, RD1 New Zealand; in Japan by T.F.H. Publications, Japan—Jiro Tsuda, 10-12-3 Ohjidai, Sakura, Chiba 285, Japan; in SOUTH AFRICA by Lopis (Pty) Ltd., P.O. Box 39127, Booysens, 2016, Johannesburg, South Africa. Published by T.F.H. Publications, Inc.
MANUFACTURED IN THE UNITED STATES OF AMERICA
BY T.F.H. PUBLICATIONS, INC.

FERRETS
IN YOUR HOME

WENDY WINSTED, M.D.

t.f.h.

Contents

INTRODUCTION

Many years ago when I got my first ferrets, they were almost unheard of as pets and kept by only a few people here and there who were especially involved with animals, and with wild animal pets in particular. Back then, whenever I took my ferrets out on the street with me in New York City, people would invariably stop and ask, "What are they?"

Things have changed considerably over the past 15 years, and ferrets have enjoyed a rapidly increasing popularity as household pets. Nowadays carrying a ferret on the street in New York City is just as likely to elicit, "Oh look, a ferret!" as it is "What is it?"

The author with two of her pet ferrets.

Many readers of my first book have written to ask how I chose to make pets of these delightful creatures and what it was, way back then, that made me think that ferrets had the potential to become popular in the future. It's a long story . . .

It started long ago in 1969 when I was working as a singer-songwriter and made my living by writing songs and traveling around the country playing college concerts, coffeehouses, and night clubs. It all sounds very glamorous, exciting and romantic on paper, and I suppose it was at first, but basically life out there "on the road" is a lonely life full of hotels and goodbyes, and when the show is over and everybody goes home, there's not much to do back in your room at the hotel. After you've watched the last five minutes of the late movie and there's nothing left but snow on your television screen, it gets pretty boring—especially since "bedtime" is at least two or three hours away. (At the end of a show most performers are usually too "hyped-up" to go to sleep for a long time afterwards, which is why, I suppose, the majority of them run on "rock and roll time," staying up all night and sleeping all day. I was no exception.)

One day in North Carolina after a particularly long and lonely night, I wandered into a local pet store and for a few moments seriously considered buying a hamster—which was at least something alive to keep me company through the long nights. I finally decided that a hamster might not be too much more entertaining than snow on the television screen, and I went back to my hotel trying to figure out if there was any way to bring my two Siamese cats along with me on my next tour. After only a few minutes of careful consideration, I remembered how loudly they

The popularity of the pet ferret has grown remarkably over the past 15 years, since the delightful personalities of these little animals have become more and more well known.

Artist's rendering of a marbled polecat, a close relative of the domestic ferret.

Armadillo: a chiefly nocturnal burrowing mammal with few or no teeth, a head and body encased in an armor of bony plates, and the ability to curl up into a ball when attacked.

meowed and I quickly abandoned the idea, as they were definitely too noisy to hide anywhere in a hotel room, and in addition, I was certain they'd go crazy on an airplane.

When I got to Chicago later that month I decided to hire a local guitarist to accompany me for a two-week club date I was playing there. One afternoon during our daily rehearsal my guitarist, Michael, and I got into a conversation about life on the road and I confessed that I'd almost gotten desperate enough to

pick up a hamster in North Carolina. He agreed that although a hamster would probably be very easy to travel with, they weren't very entertaining, and then he proceeded to tell me about a pet armadillo he'd once had.

"An armadillo would be a perfect traveling companion," he explained, "because they don't bite, they don't make any noise, and if you take them out of the house all they want to do is curl up in a ball and hide."

He also admitted that they weren't

The ermine, or stoat, along with ferrets and skunks, is a member of the family Mustilidae.

really all that much fun, and suggested that instead I consider a skunk, which he thought would be just as easy to travel with, but more interesting to watch. A skunk sounded even more promising when he told me that he'd heard they could be trained to use a litter pan, and he offered to find out where I could get one. I agreed and said I was definitely interested.

I'd almost forgotten about our conversation when I got a letter from Michael two months later with the address of an animal import farm which sold skunk kits, among other things, by mail. It turned out that they charged a lot of money for just one skunk but came down considerably on the price when you ordered more than one. When I found out that you could ship four at the same cost of shipping just one, naturally I ordered four. In New York City you can sell just about anything, so I decided to put an ad in the classified section of a local newspaper, sell three of them, keep the one I liked best and, hopefully, make enough profit to cover the cost of both the shipping and the skunk that I kept.

Sure enough, all the skunks sold almost immediately and I ended up wishing I'd ordered twice as many. More importantly, several of the people who bought skunks or called to inquire turned out to be "animal people" who were involved with and knew a lot about exotic pets; they

eventually became my good friends.

By the time Mary Bloom called there were no skunks left, but she was involved with other wild pets— she had an owl she rescued from a pet store—and although she didn't own a skunk she knew of a few people who did and was able to give me some useful information about "skunk keeping."

She told me that in order to make a good pet of a skunk you need to get it at a very young age. The ones I had gotten were nearly half grown and they were all pretty wild. (You couldn't just walk over and pick them up—you had to catch them first).

Even though my skunk, Eli, was fun to watch and wouldn't bite after you finally caught and picked him up, I decided that it would be good to have friendly skunk as well—one that I wouldn't have to catch!

Like many other wild animals living in our climate, skunks are born only in the spring, so Mary Bloom and I made arrangements to buy skunk kits from a skunk farm she knew of in Connecticut the following spring.

I named mine Sally-Michael. I got her before she opened her eyes and bottle fed her for a few weeks, so she came to look on me as her mother and was very strongly attached to me. She followed me around the house and played with me just as a kitten or puppy would.

Never leave an animal in a car with the windows rolled up—even if you park in the shade and plan to be gone only a few minutes. Shade can disappear very quickly and the car can become an oven.

True to my expectations, I found the skunks to be perfect traveling companions and always took them with me when I went out on the road; first Eli alone and later both of them. They were easily smuggled onto airplanes and into hotels because, just like Michael's armadillo, they would curl up into a ball and go to sleep, and when I zipped them up in my airline bag they didn't bark, meow, or scratch on the side to get out.

Unfortunately, Sally-Michael met an unhappy end when she was only five or six months old. I had left her with my sister to "skunk-sit" for me while I played a concert tour in Canada. Although I was pretty

crazy, I wasn't quite crazy enough to try to smuggle a couple of skunks through customs! My sister, not being an experienced animal keeper, left poor Sally-Michael in a hot car with the windows rolled up and she suffocated to death.

When I got the news I was heartbroken, and wanted to get another baby to replace her. It was early fall when she died, however, and there wouldn't be any skunks born until the following spring.

It was then that Mary Bloom suggested I get a ferret kit. "What's a ferret?" I asked. (Sound familiar?) Mary told me a little about them and said she knew of several people who had them. She said that although

Headstudy of a silver mink. Minks are resourceful animals that show some similarities to ferrets, but they cannot be considered domesticated.

she'd never actually seen one, she'd heard from people who'd had both ferrets and skunks as pets and that they made much better pets than skunks. Most importantly, I didn't have to wait until spring to get a new baby. I decided to try a ferret, thinking that I could still go ahead and get another skunk in the spring and I ordered—yes, you guessed it— four of them!

Because of my past experiences with raising wild pets (I bottle-fed a baby squirrel I found in Central Park as well as my second skunk), I specifically ordered three-week-old ferret kits. The breeder who sold me the ferrets tried to convince me that the kits would grow up just as

"tame" if they were allowed to remain with their mother until they were old enough to be weaned as they would if I "adopted" and bottle-fed them. I didn't believe him at the time (although my later experiences proved him to be right), and I insisted on obtaining infant kits.

I kept one especially dark female kit (which I named McGuinn) and sold the other three. At first I was very unimpressed with them— they still had their eyes closed and didn't do anything except drink from a bottle, sleep, and cry occasionally, and they definitely weren't as cute as a fluffy little strikingly black and white infant

"At first I was very unimpressed with them—they still had their eyes closed and didn't do anything except drink from a bottle, sleep, and cry occasionally, and they definitely weren't as cute as a fluffy little strikingly black and white infant skunk."

The practice of descenting ferrets has had major ramifications upon ferret keeping. Many people who would not have considered ferrets as pets now keep them, and those who had only one now have multiple-ferret families.

"It wasn't until they grew old enough to be playful and I discovered what truly delightful personalities they have that I became a confirmed ferret lover."

skunk. It wasn't until they grew old enough to be playful and I discovered what truly delightful personalities they have that I became a confirmed ferret lover.

By comparison the skunks were prettier and more interesting to watch, but once they reached adulthood they weren't very lively. I think a friend of mine summed it up quite accurately when he said, "They're sort of like walking plants, they *look* really nice but they don't *do* anything!" Now whenever anyone calls to ask me if I know where they can get a skunk, I always advise them to forget skunks and get a ferret—because they're at least ten times more fun!

Having had cats with kittens, rabbits with bunnies, and skunks with skunk kits, it wasn't long after getting McGuinn that I began to consider having a ferret with ferret kits. Having ferret kits, unfortunately, would create a problem.

While female ferrets have a mild and somewhat undesirable odor, male ferrets were definitely too stinky to keep as house pets. In addition, the ferret farm had (and still has) a "closed colony" policy. Once a ferret leaves the farm it is not allowed to return, and ferrets born outside the farm are not introduced into the stock. This is to ensure that a ferret from the outside does not bring in some contagious disease which potentially might spread and wipe out the entire population of the colony. This meant that if McGuinn had kits, there would almost certainly be males that couldn't be pets and couldn't be shipped to the farm. Since I refused to consider putting them to sleep, it made disposing of them a definite problem.

One day as I was sitting in my living room pondering again upon how and/or where to get rid of male ferret kits, Eli, another stinky member of the ferret family, happened to wander across my view. It suddenly occurred to me that skunks couldn't be house pets without being descented, and since I knew that ferrets, like skunks, have large anal glands, I wondered if perhaps descenting ferrets might provide a solution to the odor problem.

Excited, I called a veterinarian friend, Dr. Paul Cavanaugh, who had descented several skunks, and asked him what he thought about the idea. He said he'd never heard of anyone descenting a ferret, but agreed it was worth a try.

One evening the following week I watched him descent a young female I had on hand to be sold, and then, with him standing by directing me, I descented McGuinn. (At the time I was working part-time for my skunk's veterinarian and had a considerable amount of experience doing surgery on cats.)

After being descented and given a bath, McGuinn had no more odor than a cat and considerably less odor than a dog (especially a wet one!), so when she came into heat I ordered a stud for her and a few days after breeding them, I descented him. While descenting seemed to render him a little less odoriferous, he was still too offensive for the house, so I decided to see if neutering him would make any additional improvement. Fortunately it did, and when both castrated and descented he had no more odor than McGuinn did. When McGuinn's kits arrived I descented them and neutered the males and all of them happily became house pets.

In the years that followed I continued descenting ferrets, and I believe that the ramifications of this practice have been enormous. I have always had a strong suspicion that one of the reasons that ferrets never became popular pets in the past was because of their offensive odor, and subsequently that their present popularity is, aside from the attraction of their delightful, friendly personalities, the result of the elimination of this odor problem.

In the next few years after descenting McGuinn I visited several of the major ferret farms in the United States and taught my technique for descenting ferrets. (Different than the method used for descenting skunks, the technique I

"I have always had a strong suspicion that one of the reasons that ferrets never became popular pets in the past was because of their offensive odor, and subsequently that their present popularity is, aside from the attraction of their delightful, friendly personalities, the result of the elimination of this odor problem."

The author's ferrets are shown here with their ferret sitter, Dr. Norma Wagoner, Dean of Students at Cincinnati College of Medicine. The ferrets usually went to class with their owner, but at times when classes were held in the hospital they played in Dr. Wagoner's office instead.

use is extremely simple and evolved gradually through repetition of the procedure on several thousand ferrets.) Ferret breeders, in turn, began to sell descented ferrets, and the popularity of the ferret began to grow as more and more people became acquainted with these fun-loving little clowns who no longer had to hide out in the garage because they were in continual need of a bath.

One of the many things I like about ferrets is that, like skunks, they are good travelers. They are small and quiet (they don't bark or meow when smuggled onto airplanes), and readily adapt to almost anything. As a singer-songwriter I took my ferrets out on the road with me when I went on tour, and they seemed to enjoy it so much that I ended up taking them with me wherever I went in town as well—shopping, movies, nightclubs, and even to restaurants.

As time went on I became disenchanted with my "traveling troubador" life, and I began to look around for an alternative to being on the road. My interest in skunk and ferret medicine and surgery led me to working as a veterinary technician, and consequently I

These three buddies look like they're engaged in some kind of mischief.

developed an interest in medicine in general. I decided to go to college and earn a degree—in hopes of eventually getting into medical school.

Because I was in the habit of having my ferrets with me wherever I went, I took Melinda and McGuinn to school with me every day of the five years I attended undergraduate classes at Brooklyn and Hunter Colleges. Later, after McGuinn died, Melinda and Sally continued to accompany me to class through my first two years of medical school. They rode in my shoulder bag—which was big enough to be my purse and bookbag as well as their mobile home, complete with litter pan and bed.

During the lectures they would curl up and sleep quietly, having learned long ago that the classroom was not a place where they were allowed to get down and walk around, but rather a boring place where someone stood up in the front of the room and talked for what must have seemed to them like an inordinately long amount of time. Sometimes it seemed like an inordinately long amount of time even to me, and there were many times when I honestly wished that they would stay awake and take notes for a change while I curled up and went to sleep!

My little pets were so quiet and

well behaved in the classroom that most of the students weren't even aware of their presence. (My endocrinology professor did not notice that I always had one or two of them sleeping on my lap until the last day of classes—and I always sat in the front row!) It was understandable, consequently, that it was well into the middle of the semester before Iris Ramirez, a pre-veterinary student in my chemistry class at Brooklyn College, noticed them sleeping in my lap.

Iris was immediately taken with my little pets and started sitting next to me in class so that either Melinda or McGuinn could sleep on her lap. By the end of the week she decided she had to have a ferret of her own to bring to class, and conveniently enough it happened that I was working my way through school by selling ferrets.

I arranged to bring her a cute little White-footed kit on the following Monday. She arrived at the appointed time in the hallway outside the classroom—fully equipped with a shoulder bag mobile home for her new pet and excited about the prospect of having a traveling companion of her very own.

As I took the kit out of my bag and handed it to Iris, she voiced her concern: "I'm afraid she'll jump out of my bag. She's not trained like

"Because I was in the habit of having my ferrets with me wherever I went, I took Melinda and McGuinn to school with me every day of the five years I attended undergraduate classes at Brooklyn and Hunter Colleges."

"I find it much safer to say 'most ferrets don't,' or 'most ferrets usually don't,' because as soon as you say 'never' there's likely to be one right there to prove you a liar."

Melinda and McGuinn."

"Melinda and McGuinn are trained not to jump out of my bag just like you're trained not to jump out of a three-story window!" I assured her. "Just watch her to see that she doesn't lean over the edge too far in her curiosity to see what's going on and accidentally fall. She may fall but she won't jump. Ferrets don't jump."

By this time it was almost time for class to commence, so Iris gently placed the kit in her shoulder bag and we started walking down the hall toward the classroom door. I'm sure we had gone all of three steps when Iris's new kit gathered itself up and then did not merely jump but literally leaped up and out into mid-air. It crashed to the floor with a thud that must have knocked all the wind out of the poor little youngster and lay spread-eagle and motionless on the floor—stunned but uninjured.

It was the first time I'd ever seen a ferret jump, and at that time I'd had my ferrets for several years and sold over 100 kits. It was also the last time I ever said "ferrets don't." I find it much safer to say "most ferrets don't," or "most ferrets usually don't," because as soon as you say "never" there's likely to be one right there to prove you a liar.

Unfortunately, I made this discovery after writing my first book about ferrets rather than before. No sooner did I put down the "facts" for all the world to read than sure enough, a few of the "facts" changed. For example, in my first book I said: "Unlike cats, most ferrets get along well together from the first time they meet. I have never seen ferrets fight when introduced to one another—they usually appear to be overjoyed to see each other and begin to play almost immediately." This was certainly true when I wrote it, but only a few days after the ink

dried on the first printing of *Ferrets*, which was published by T.F.H. as a part of their KW series, both Melinda and McGuinn began fighting with every ferret they met, and at about the same time I started getting reports of other ferrets who were exhibiting similar behavior. Since then, one of the most frequent inquiries I receive from readers of the first book concerns how to introduce a new ferret into the household with a minimum amount of fussing and fighting!

In the years that *Ferrets* has been available in pet stores, both in the United States and in numerous other countries, many readers have called or written me with questions about other things I'd failed to mention. In the meantime I learned more about ferrets and thought of other little bits and pieces of information I would have liked to have included in my first book.

This omitted material and the changing "facts" have led me to write this book, in which I necessarily include some of the same basic information contained in my first book, although in somewhat greater detail and in a slightly different form.

I hope this new book will entertain you as well as provide you with a practical guide to keeping a ferret as a house pet, and that it will help you to enjoy your little pet.

I would like to thank Dr. Constance Martin for her help with the sections on reproduction, and veterinarians Emil Dolensek, Thomas Kawasaki, Michael Leis, W.B. Nelson, Laurence Reeve, and L.M. Ryland, for their help with the section on health. Thanks also to veterinarians Thomas Angel, Len Britt, John Gorham, Richard Novick, and C.W. Schaubhut, and to Chuck and Fox Morton, Dr. Damon Miller, Mary Bloom and Gary Kaskel for their contributions.

As the popularity of the ferret continues to grow, more and more information about this unique animal is discovered. Veterinarians researching the physiology of the ferret continue to gain insight into its anatomy, and pet owners make discoveries of their own concerning diet, personality, and individual preferences.

CHOOSING YOUR FERRET

Once you've decided that a ferret is the ideal pet, the next step is to choose the one that's right for you. People often call me and ask such questions as: "Which makes a better pet, a male or a female?"; "Is one color more gentle or friendly than another?"; "If I get a young kit will he become more attached to me than an older one?"

Unfortunately, there are no definite answers to these questions. Ferrets seem to be a lot like people in that how nice they are depends on their inherent personality and upbringing rather than on their age, sex or color. When the time comes to pick your pet out of a group or litter, you will have to rely on intuition. Aside from such influencing factors as fur color or sex, a pet's personality can only be revealed gradually through time.

MALE OR FEMALE?

The sex of the animal really shouldn't present a dilemma. Males and females both make excellent pets. The only difference is size and weight. Not including the tail, a male will generally average about sixteen inches in length. His weight will be around three pounds, giving him a slightly wider torso than the female, which will average one and a half pounds. Female lengths average fourteen inches, only slightly smaller than the male. The large weight difference between sexes is apparent in their faces: females have thin faces with delicately pointed snouts, while males are broad-faced with more rounded snouts. I have always preferred females because, due to their small size, they are more portable and fit easily into my handbag, enabling me to take them with me wherever I go. Many people prefer males because they find the larger size more attractive.

It is interesting to note that some major breeders are currently working to produce even larger ferrets, both male and female, and it is quite possible that in the future the average ferret will be considerably larger than the ferret of today. Many ferret owners agree that this is desirable because, although ferrets don't really look much like rodents, some people equate "little and brown" with "rodent," a larger breed could conceivably help to take ferrets out of the guinea pig and rat category, where they are still often wrongly placed.

Choosing a pet ferret is not a decision to be taken lightly. Consider the color and sex of the ferret before you make a purchase, and, of course, be sure to choose a healthy ferret.

Health and good temperament are the most important characteristics to consider when choosing a pet ferret, while sex and color are a matter of choice.

Siamese markings: dark markings that are usually found on the extremities of an animal, often called the Himalayan pattern.

If you are cost conscious, one factor which may influence your choice of gender is the considerably higher cost of spaying the female over castrating the male. The female's surgical cost is generally double the male's. This neutering operation is a must (unless you plan to breed your pet) both for health reasons and odor control.

COLOR

For most people, coat color and markings are important considerations when it comes to choosing a ferret. A ferret's fur is made up of two types of hair, an inner layer or undercoat, consisting of very fine textured, soft, short fur, and an outer layer of coarser guard hairs. These guard hairs are considerably longer than the undercoat except on the feet, legs, face, ears, and tip of the tail, where they become short and close cropped and where the soft downy undercoat is absent. Except in the White and White-footed ferrets, the majority of the guard hairs are a darker color than the undercoat, and because of the absence of the light undercoat on the feet, legs, and tail, these areas appear darker than the rest of the body. This, along with dark ears and the "raccoon-like" mask across the eyes gives the ferret the typical "Siamese" markings. These Siamese markings can be either subtle or

striking, depending on the overall coloring of the animal.

The most common color is the Sable ferret, which has a light beige undercoat and dark brown guard hairs. The darkest variation of the Sable is sometimes called the McGuinn Sable, or the Ranch Sable, and has very dark brown to black guard hairs with a pale beige undercoat. Another variation of the Sable has the same dark brown guard hairs, but the undercoat is more golden-yellowish than beige

The coat of most ferret color varieties is made up of a light undercoat and darker guard hairs.

No matter what color ferret you choose, he should be alert and aware of his surroundings.

and is called Honey Sable.

A third variation of the Sable is the Butterscotch, formerly called Siamese. These ferrets have the same markings as the Sable, but their guard hairs are a lighter tan instead of dark brown or black. Since all ferrets, except for the Albino, Red-eyed White, and White-footed ferrets, have darker legs, tails, and ears than the rest of the body, they all essentially have "Siamese" markings and the name Siamese tends to be confusing. As a consequence, the name Butterscotch was recently chosen by several of the major breeders to replace the designation "Siamese."

White-footed ferrets, sometimes called Silver Mitts, are another color variation with white feet or legs. In addition, they usually have a white bib under the neck. A few have white spots or streaks on top of the head or on the back, or a white tip on the tail. White-footed ferrets come in various shades ranging from the very dark, like the Sable, to light tan. Hence you may have a White-footed Sable, White-footed Honey Sable, a White-footed McGuinn Sable, or a White-footed Butterscotch. The White-footed ferrets also have a dark mask across the eyes.

Silver ferrets have some white

Albino: an animal that is deficient or devoid of pigmentation, characterized by white body coloration and pink eyes; a true albino cannot pass on genes for any other color.

This is Moseley, one of the author's ferrets.

Guard hairs: a coat of long, coarse hairs that form a protective layer over the underfur of an animal, often of a different color than the undercoat.

guard hairs mixed in with their dark brown or tan guard hairs, always have white feet, and frequently have a white bib. Both the Silver and the White-footed colorings have less pronounced facial markings than the Sable varieties.

Another common color is the Red-eyed White ferret. Although frequently called an Albino, the majority of these animals are not true Albinos. This is apparent when breeding two of them together. If they were true Albinos, which is a genetically recessive trait, one would

expect to get only Albino offspring. This is seldom the case, however, and more frequently the offspring are a mixture of Red-eyed Whites and other colors.

The Black-eyed White ferret, an offshoot of the Red-eyed White, is quite common in Australia. However, they are just beginning to be produced in the United States, and are still quite rare.

One of the newer colors, a variation of the Silver, is the Sterling Silver, which has more white guard hairs than the standard Silver mixed

in with black guard hairs. Like the Silver it also has a light undercoat and white feet, and usually has a much less pronounced mask. At a distance this ferret appears pale gray.

Another of the newer colors is the Cinnamon ferret, which is a variation of the Butterscotch. Its guard hairs are a cinnamon colored light tan with a definite reddish cast, and its undercoat is a very light whitish beige. Like the Silver it also usually has less prominent facial markings.

For each color designation there is a wide range in the shades of color of both the guard hairs and the undercoat, so that not all the Butterscotch ferrets, for example,

will be exactly the same color, and so on.

Now that ferrets are being bred for pets rather than exclusively as research animals as they were in the past, more attention has been turned to color and body conformation as well as temperament, and consequently we can expect to see even more new colors in the future.

When choosing a kit, remember that it takes time for the guard hairs to grow out to the adult color and for the beige undercoat to appear, so unless you buy an older ferret it is very difficult, if not impossible, to tell exactly what shade of color the animal is going to be as an adult, other than the major color designation, such as Sable or Butterscotch. Color, temperament, and personality are not related, and a Sable is no more or less gentle, wild, or friendly than a Red-eyed White or any other color.

MASKS

One of the most distinctive features of ferrets is the facial mask. This becomes visible at about two to three weeks of age. Twin patches of white fur form beneath the ears. As the animal grows and matures, these light patches spread and thicken in the area above and around the eyes. These contrasting colors of the ferret's mask change with the

Individual ferrets may show differences in the growth of their facial masks from season to season, but the most drastic differences are caused by sterilization. Once a ferret is altered, it will usually not grow another full mask.

Body conformation: the overall shape and proportions of an animal's body, often affected by selective breeding.

As ferret breeding continues to grow in popularity, more new color varieties will be created. In addition, old ones will continue to be perfected.

"All ferrets seem to enjoy the company of people. Some, however, can become exceptionally 'people oriented.' "

seasons. In general, during the winter months, the white patch of facial fur increases and thickens, as does the entire coat. This gives the animal his "full mask." During the warm months, the fur thins and darkens. The white in most cases will recede back into small twin patches below the ears.

You may not notice such a range of contrast in facial color if your pet has been neutered. McGuinn, for example, grew a thick mask during her first winter. I had her spayed during the summer. During the following winter, the changes in facial mask color and thickness were much less pronounced. Many altered ferrets, both male and female, do not grow a full mask in the winter or the summer. Even if they are left out in the cold weather, their coats usually don't become quite as thick as unaltered animals. This is because coat growth is affected by sex hormone levels.

FORMING ATTACHMENTS

Although a young kit may become more quickly attached to you than an older animal, age is not of primary importance in selecting a satisfactory pet. If shown a generous amount of attention and affection, a ferret with an agreeable disposition will develop a close attachment to you.

All ferrets seem to enjoy the company of people. Some, however, can become exceptionally "people oriented." The reasons for this human closeness are totally unclear. I received my first ferret, McGuinn, when she was three and a half weeks old. In the hopes of developing an extremely close attachment, I bottle-fed her for three weeks, serving as a surrogate mother. This type of hand-rearing is usually employed with wild animals in order to gain some degree of human acceptance. Hand-reared animals from the woods will develop a friendship only with the person who has acted as the surrogate mother.

A year later I purchased my second ferret, Melinda. At ten weeks of age, she was well past the age of dependence on a surrogate mother. She was extremely shy the first few days. She ran and hid under the refrigerator whenever I approached to pick her up. But after a period of adjustment she became closer and more affectionate than McGuinn had ever been. When she finished playing, she would routinely curl up in my lap and sleep. McGuinn, my hand-reared orphan, preferred to nap under the sofa or in the laundry hamper. As time went on, McGuinn also came to sleep on my lap, but only if Melinda was already there. It

All ferrets will become attached to their owners to some degree; however, some ferrets are naturally more affectionate than others.

seemed that bottle-feeding and hand-raising, in this case, didn't have any overwhelming influence on McGuinn. She was not a wild animal pet; therefore the surrogate mother bond obviously didn't affect her in the same manner.

Three years later I acquired Sally, who was already over a year old. Prior to this, she had lived in an outdoor cage and had never been handled. I chose her rather than a young kit because of her intriguing markings and body conformation. She was obviously a McGuinn Silver Mitt, and because she was fully developed at one year, her appearance and markings would probably remain. She had a very short, broad face and almost stubbed nose, which was unusual in a female. Her white, clear-cut feet contrasted sharply with her exceptionally dark body.

I thought I was going to be in for some definite pan-training problems as a result of her outdoor cage upbringing. Surprisingly, this was not the case. She became pan-trained with the ease of any other average ferret. She had a shy temperament similar to that of a new kit. I believe that this shyness would have been overcome sooner if she had been an "only pet." Being the third in line, she never received as much attention as had McGuinn and Melinda.

PET QUALITY

When you purchase a ferret it is important to make sure that you are getting pet quality stock. Regardless of age, sex, and color, you should look for one that has been bred to be gentle and docile. The health of your new pet is equally important. He should be alert and active and his eyes should be bright and clear. His nose and eyes should be free of crust and discharge. Observe the coat and whiskers; a thin, dry coat with broken stubby whiskers is a sign of possible coccidiosis, a disease that can cause severe diarrhea, debilitation and possible death in young animals.

TEMPERAMENT AND HANDLING

"If you find that you need to wear gloves when you handle your kit because he is consistently biting you hard enough to draw blood, you are not getting pet-quality stock and you should probably look elsewhere for a pet."

When you are ready to purchase a ferret it is advisable to shop around until you find a pet shop that sells pet-quality animals. There is a vast difference between ferrets raised for research and by fur farms (to make coats) and ferrets selectively bred to be docile and gentle, good-natured pets. If you find that you need to wear gloves when you handle your kit because he is consistently biting you hard enough to draw blood, you are not getting pet-quality stock and you should probably look elsewhere for a pet.

Most of the ferrets which have been raised specifically for the purpose of being pets are the product of selective breeding over several generations. Because biting and bad temperament are inherited characteristics, ferrets that tend to bite are culled and not used for breeding—instead only docile animals are mated together. In addition, the offspring of two gentle ferrets who turn out to have had the biting trait passed down to them from their grandparents, great grandparents, or great-great-great grandparents are likewise culled. The result is that after enough generations have been born from "selected" animals, the offspring no longer contain the genetic material to produce ferrets with nasty temperaments and the tendency to bite. Although these selectively bred pet-quality ferrets cost more than fur farm ferrets, they are usually well worth the money.

Over the years, numerous ferret owners have called or written me to say that their pet is friendly and easy to handle until he gets tired and no longer wants to play or be picked up, at which time he turns around and bites them quite hard and viciously, drawing blood. Several of these same ferret owners have asked what they are doing wrong, assuming that they must be making some mistake in the manner in

Most ferrets love the idea of digging up a potted plant. To protect your flora from horticultural ferrets and your fauna from poisonous plants, keep your plants out of reach of your ferrets.

26

Most of the ferrets on the market today have been bred for good temperament. If you own a bad-tempered ferret, do not use it for breeding, since doing so will only perpetuate an unwanted characteristic in future ferret generations.

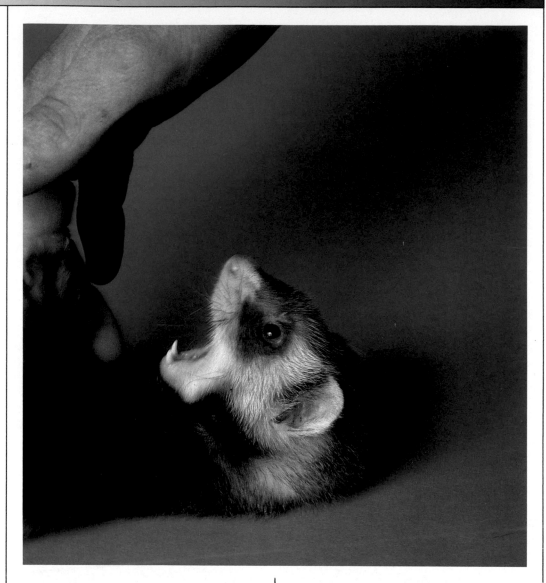

Most young ferrets that nip do so because they have not learned to distinguish between what is food and what is not. This does not necessarily mean that such a kit has a bad temperament.

"In order to avoid getting bitten, it is advisable to note when and under what circumstances this type of ill-tempered ferret is likely to bite, and then avoid handling him at those times."

which they handle or play with their ferret that is causing such vicious behavior. The problem in these cases is not the owner, but the ferret. This is a good example of a bad-tempered animal.

In order to avoid getting bitten it is advisable to note when and under what circumstances this type of ill-tempered ferret is likely to bite, and then avoid handling him at those times. Never use an ill-tempered ferret for breeding.

YOUNG FERRETS

Baby ferrets may also occasionally nip too hard in playing with you. It may take them a while to learn just how hard they can chomp on your finger without hurting you. After

all, until you took them home, the only experience they had had in playing and wrestling had probably been with other ferrets who have tough, leathery skin compared to yours. A nip on a littermate's leg may hardly be felt, while a chew of the same magnitude on your finger may hurt! How is the little fellow to know this until you tell him?

He may get the idea if you just screech or holler when he gets too rough. If he chews or hangs on, a little spank on the rear flank or a thump on the nose will usually cause him to release your finger immediately. After a few minutes he will probably get the idea and play with you a little more gently. Don't spank him on top of the head; this will only pound his teeth deeper into your finger. Remember that you are spanking a tiny animal and use the appropriate amount of force—don't beat him to death! Also be sure that the spank occurs while his teeth are actually on you and not afterward when he won't be able to relate the spank to the nip.

Again, it is important to stress that while these nips and bites may be a little painful, they usually won't break the skin and are no more than you would expect from a kitten or puppy. There is a great deal of difference between these nips and the hard bite that consistently draws blood and requires the protection of gloves. Anyone should be able to safely handle a good pet-quality, well-fed kit, assuming the handling is done gently and quietly and without frightening the animal.

BITTER APPLE

If you have a kit who continues to nip and play too rough despite frequent scoldings and spankings, or if you find that, like some ferret owners, you just don't have the heart to spank your little pet, you may wish to discourage his nipping habit by using Bitter Apple, a product which can be obtained at your local pet store. It comes in a spray bottle and has a taste which most animals find very unpleasant. Some ferret owners say that they've found it to be quite effective if sprayed in the animal's mouth and face when he is in the middle of a nip, and they report that after using it for a few days to a few weeks, depending on the animal, their pet learned not to be so rough in playing with them and the nipping habit ceased.

FANG REMOVAL

Many owners of bad-tempered ferrets, who have gotten tired of having painful bites inflicted upon them, frequently ask me if I recommend fang removal as a solution to this problem. I feel that while this can be done by an experienced veterinarian without any severe harm to the animal, it is not a good idea. In addition to being a very drastic measure to have to take, it is usually not too effective because ferrets, like other animals who have had their canine teeth or "fangs" removed, can usually do just as much damage with the teeth they have remaining, the incisors and molars. I believe that the owner of such a bad-tempered animal could do much better if he spent the money he would have used for fang removal (which is usually an expensive procedure) to purchase a good, pet-quality ferret, which he will enjoy much more in the long run. The biting ferret need not be abandoned, but can instead be kept as a companion for the nicer, pet-quality ferret.

"Anyone should be able to safely handle a good pet-quality, well-fed kit, assuming the handling is done gently and quietly and without frightening the animal."

A genetically sound ferret should never object to proper handling.

"Biting and nasty temperament seem to be dominant rather than recessive traits, and if you cross a biter with a docile, pet-quality ferret it is quite possible to get an entire litter of babies who bite."

THE HUMANE SOCIETY

Another alternative is to give him to someone who will accept him for the ferret he is and who will tolerate an occasional bite. Owning this type of animal is a little like owning a wild pet or a nervous dog—you can never totally rely on him not to bite. Like a wild pet or nervous dog, an ill-tempered ferret should *not* be part of a family with young children.

If you decide that you have a ferret that you just can't keep for one reason or another, please remember that a ferret is *not* a wild animal and should never be turned loose in the woods. He will be unable to survive and will probably die a painful and unhappy death. If you are unable to find another home for him you should call your local humane society, which will either take him or advise you about what to do with him.

I would also urge you *not* to use an ill-tempered animal for breeding purposes. Biting and nasty temperament seem to be dominant rather than recessive traits, and if you cross a biter with a docile, pet-quality ferret it is quite possible to get an entire litter of babies who bite. If you wish to breed ferrets it is a good idea to purchase good stock and perpetuate desirable, rather than undesirable, characteristics. Selling ferret kits that bite (especially to people who don't know that ferrets *shouldn't* bite!) will only help to give ferrets a bad reputation. In addition, it is reasonable to ask a higher price for good natured, pet-quality ferrets. A cheap ferret usually isn't a bargain at all and quite likely will not make a good pet!

NIPPING

There is a big difference between nipping and serious biting, and like all baby animals (even baby people!) some ferret kits nip. If these kits are from pet-quality stock, however, they will eventually outgrow this nipping stage.

Baby animals nip for several reasons, and ferret babies are no exception. First of all, a very young baby probably has been weaned just recently. It is used to getting milk from its mother and is still learning to eat food from a dish. It takes a little experience before the kit figures out exactly what is food and what is not food. In addition to trying to eat your finger, he is likely to try to eat the dish or spoon as well as the food that is in it. A hungry kit, especially one from a large litter, may have gotten into the habit of competing with littermates for food and will consequently grab or bite something first and then check later (when he's gotten it away from other kits) to see if it's food. You can help by feeding him before you handle him, but even then he may still want to nurse and may try your finger. Fortunately, most kits are not too aggressive about this, but it is best to handle them in a manner that will keep your hand out of the range of their sharp tiny teeth.

HANDLING

The best way to pick up a kit is to distract him with one hand while you pick him up with the other. Approaching him from behind, grasp him with your thumb and index finger around his neck, with the other three fingers behind his front legs and under his chest. Then use your other hand to support his rear legs. Never dangle your fingers in front of him, as he is likely to see them as play things to be attacked and caught. Needless to say, *never* pick up a ferret by his tail!

DESCENTING

The ferret is a close cousin of the skunk, and both are members of the family Mustelidae, along with the otter, mink, weasel, marten, and badger. All members of this family have two anal glands, or "scent glands," one on each side of the rectum. These glands consist of little sacs, or pouches, which are about ¾ of an inch long by ½ an inch wide in the average adult male ferret, and somewhat smaller in the female. They contain a thick, yellowish, foul smelling fluid known as *musk*. The family name Mustelidae, incidentally, is derived from the Latin word for musk.

The skunk, which produces by far the strongest and most unpleasant smelling musk of any member of the family, is famous for his ability to spray this fluid, which he does only as a defense against would-be predators. Other family members, including the ferret, are unable to spray; however, they can excrete several drops of musk at a time, and will readily do so when frightened or upset.

These same scent glands also contribute to the ferret's strong "musky" smell which begins as a mild odor in a young kit and increases as the animal (especially a male) matures.

Many cute, cuddly baby ferrets have been purchased by people who never realized that as the animals grew, so did their odor. Ferrets when fully grown are downright "stinkers." A small percentage of owners do tolerate the strong musky smell, but they'll probably admit that folks just don't seem to drop by for a visit anymore. Many owners have not been so tolerant of the smell. Thus, many ferrets have been doomed by their own natural scent. The once-loved pet is stuck in a backyard cage or, worse yet, abandoned entirely to the horrors of the woods.

Unfortunately, banishing the smelly ferret to the backyard doesn't

completely solve the odor problem. Owners who handle the animals will still come away smelling of ferret. The odor is powerful. It settles and lingers on hands and clothing. Bathing the animal will help for only a short time. In a matter of days, the odor will be back in full force. The only wise solution to the problem is descenting.

THE OPERATION

Descenting a ferret is a procedure in which the animal is anesthetized and the anal glands are surgically removed, using a technique similar to the one used for descenting a skunk. This descenting operation will drastically reduce the odor, provided that the surgically treated ferret is a female, and she is not in heat. The sex hormones also play a role in odor production, and descenting alone is not adequate for odor control in the male, even if he is not in season. Descenting helps, but both descenting and castration (which removes the source of the male sex hormone, testosterone) are

Family: a taxonomical group of animals or plants that are related by common characteristics, ranking above genus and below order.

Many pet shops and breeders are beginning to sell altered and descented ferrets.

needed to eliminate the strong musky smell of the male.

Descenting will eliminate all but a lingering trace of musk odor. If you have a sensitive nose, frequent bathing of the neutered, descented animal will keep him virtually odor free.

BUYING A DESCENTED FERRET

To avoid headaches, it is best to buy your ferret from a pet dealer or breeder who sells descented and castrated kits. Many pet shops also sell spayed female kits. The expense of purchasing a kit with the surgery all completed will be higher. In the long run, however, you will save money. If your heart is set on a ferret that has not yet been

descented, have the surgery done by an experienced veterinarian. Because of the increasing popularity of ferrets as pets, more and more veterinarians are becoming familiar with this surgical procedure. Most vets who descent skunks will descent ferrets. The important thing to bear in mind is that descenting and castration or descenting and spaying should both be done at an early age, preferably six to eight weeks. The rapid growth rate at this young age will assure fast, complete healing. Both surgical procedures can and should be done at the same time for convenience and cost.

If you have an unfortunate stinky two-year-old out in the garage, it's not too late, however, because ferrets in good health can be

descented at any age.

It is preferable to do both the neutering and descenting at the same time because the ferret is anesthetized and put through the ordeal of surgery only once rather than twice. Many people, as well as numerous veterinarians, have been concerned that early neutering may change the growth pattern or predispose the animal to certain diseases or health problems, such as renal calculi in the male. It has been my experience in the past ten years of having this surgery performed on young kits, and also the experience of numerous veterinarians across the country, that early neutering has no effect on the ultimate size, growth pattern, health or personality of a ferret. There are at present no contraindications to such early surgery.

If you are unable to locate a veterinarian to descent your ferret, you'd be better off purchasing a female, as they have a somewhat milder odor than males and some people are able to tolerate them undescented if they are given frequent baths. The females however, will still have a much stronger odor during the time that they are in heat and while pregnant and nursing kits, and may smell just as offensive as the males do at these times.

PREPARING FOR ARRIVAL

Before you bring your new ferret home, you'll want to have everything set up and ready for him so that his transition from the pet store or breeder to his new home is as easy as possible—for both of you. You will want to make sure you have "ferret-proofed" the house and that you have the following things ready.

CAGES

You should not simply let the ferret loose in the house after he is first brought home. He will most likely be frightened and disoriented because of the immensity of his new environment. His instinct will be to hide for long periods, and ferrets are quite good at that. He will slip into nooks and crannies that you never thought existed, and consequently a cage is the best dwelling area for him at this time. With a cage, his whereabouts will be known and you will have a much easier time pan-training him.

When considering what type of cage to get, keep in mind its most important function: to keep the ferret inside. If you decide to go with a store-bought cage, it may be wise to observe your ferret inside and make sure he can't find a way out before you make your purchase final. Ferrets can squeeze through very small spaces and may be able to escape from a cage that looks as if it would hold them.

If you are considering a wooden cage, think twice. Wood readily absorbs the odors of urine, musk, and excrement. Despite your efforts to scrub out the smell, a trace of it may linger. This scent may attract a ferret to the same spot repeatedly, thereby creating a toilet area where you do not want one. If you're stuck with a wooden cage, this odor absorption can be overcome by applying several thick coats of high-gloss polyurethane to the wood.

You should exercise common sense in selecting a cage that will be roomy enough for your pet (who may be rapidly growing). For the cage material, standard one by one-inch or one by two-inch welded wire will suffice. To enable easy access and cleaning of the cage floor, record the bottom area dimensions and design a tray that can be slid in and out of the cage. A sheet-metal shop will build a tray according to your specifications. By including a one to four-inch (the higher the better) lip or side around this base tray, the outside area near the cage will be much easier to keep clean.

Galvanized steel is the cheapest metal you can use to make a tray; however, this will eventually rust if not kept completely dry at all times. Stainless steel, while considerably more expensive, is nicer looking, will never rust, and lasts virtually forever.

Another alternative for the tray bottom is Plexiglas®. You can either buy the pieces cut to size and glue them together yourself, or at most places you can just specify the size and the shop will put it together for you. The cost is usually somewhat intermediate between galvanized steel and stainless steel. It has the disadvantage of eventually coming unglued after several years of use and can also get broken.

Probably the cheapest alternative for a tray bottom is to use a giant sized cat litter pan, which is easily obtained at your local pet store. Sometimes it is difficult, however, to find one with straight rather than sloping sides. One of the

For practical reasons, pet shops commonly house several ferrets together, placing shavings on the bottom of the cage instead of using a litter pan. When buying your ferret at a pet shop, it is a good idea to purchase the cage and a litter pan at the same time.

disadvantages of using a jumbo litter pan for a tray bottom is that you have to build the cage to conform to the size of the pan, rather than being able to choose the size cage you want and designing a tray to fit.

If you are building your own cage you may wish to design it so that the tray bottom does not cover the entire cage—and instead leave a space for the litter pan so that, much like the piece to a puzzle, it fits snugly into the bottom of the cage rather than sitting inside the tray. If the sides of the tray bottom are high enough, it will hold the litter pan firmly in place and help prevent young kits (as well as older ferrets) from moving it around the cage or overturning it.

Whether buying or building your own cage, avoid one with a wire bottom or wire flooring, as this will make pan-training your ferret extremely difficult, if not impossible. If your ferret can relieve himself anywhere in the cage and

have his mess fall through the wire where he doesn't have to walk in it or deal with it, he will have no incentive whatsoever to use the litter pan—and probably won't.

You may want to pan-train your ferret and let him roam loose in the house. If so, you may not need an elaborate, expensive cage. However, your pet should have some type of cage or dwelling for temporary usage. A big cardboard box such as one used for paper towels is suitable for this purpose. It is light, inexpensive, and easy to cut. The only drawback is the occasional need to replace the entire box. The pet's dwelling should always be as clean and litter-free as possible, and cardboard generally does not stand up well to constant soiling and cleaning without shredding or loosening. It will also absorb an increasing amount of odor.

For short periods, a bathtub can be used as a temporary dwelling,

No matter what type of cage you plan to keep your ferret in, be sure to let him out for adequate exercise and recreation.

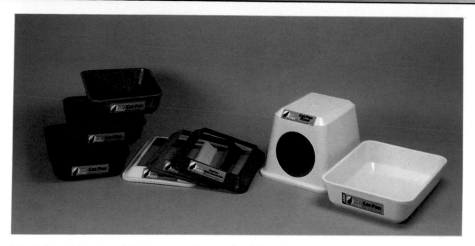

The litter pan that you select for your ferret should be sturdy, durable, and easy to clean. Photo courtesy of Hagen.

provided the sides are high enough. In case your ferret might be endowed with Olympic high-jump potential, remember to close the bathroom door. This ounce of prevention may possibly save you an involved clean up of the house, following the lengthy search for your escaped ferret. In addition, since it is difficult, if not impossible, to attach a water bottle to the side of the tub, you will need to have a heavy water dish which your pet cannot overturn. While it may seem like a good idea to just leave the water

dripping slowly from the tap in order to provide fresh water, I found out the hard way just how dangerous this can be when I was visiting my friends David and Linda Carradine in Malibu, California, and used their bath tub for a temporary ferret cage.

I didn't have the ferrets' water dish with me, so I cleverly left the faucet dripping to provide a constant source of fresh water. Linda, David, and I went out to the beach for a swim on the first day and came home several hours later to find my six ferrets, including Sally's three five-week-old babies, doing some swimming of their own. Their bedding had gotten pushed down over the drain, stopping it up, and the tub was completely filled with water. I don't know how long they had been swimming but they were unable to climb out and the babies were crying and gasping for air and they were all very tired. I'm certain that if I'd discovered them much later some, if not all, of them would eventually have drowned!

A shower stall can be used as a temporary cage provided that it has a tight-latching door. This is especially convenient in that, like the bathtub, it is quite easily washed.

A BED

Any small shallow container such as a cut-down cardboard box or basket will serve nicely as a bed. If you use a small basket, you may

"For short periods, a bathtub can be used as a temporary dwelling, provided the sides are high enough. In case your ferret might be endowed with Olympic high-jump potential, remember to close the bathroom door."

Actor David Carradine holding the author's ferret McGuinn.

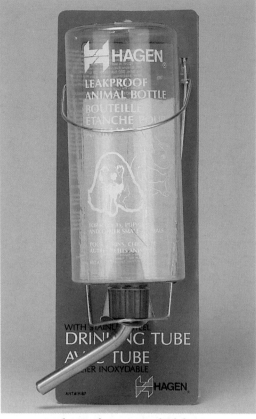

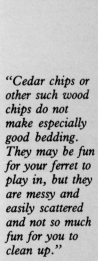

"Cedar chips or other such wood chips do not make especially good bedding. They may be fun for your ferret to play in, but they are messy and easily scattered and not so much fun for you to clean up."

want to hang it suspended by a rope or some strings from the top of the cage or attach it to the side of the cage with some wire so that your pet can walk around underneath it. This will give your ferret more space in his cage, as well as giving him some exercise when he climbs into and out of bed. In addition, some ferrets just seem to enjoy such a sleeping arrangement. At one time I had a basket on the floor of my ferrets' cage as well as a hanging basket, and the hanging bed was always the most popular place to sleep, although I'm not sure what the attraction to it was—maybe they liked the "swing" effect.

A birdhouse can be used to create a unique, fun-filled sleeping area. Make sure the entrance hole is at least two inches wide for a female, three inches wide for a full sized male. Ferrets will delight themselves by slipping in and out the small hole. Pet stores also sell disposable cardboard birdhouses. They can provide an inexpensive solution to the problem of odor build up.

Although it won't last as long, a shoe box and attached top will provide a good ferret bedroom. Just cut a hole in the side. The top can be opened to periodically change the bedding material. The bedding, which consists of clean towels, rags, or scrap cloth, should be changed every few days or more often, depending upon the amount of odor build up.

Cedar chips or other such wood chips do not make especially good bedding. They may be fun for your ferret to play in, but used as bedding they are messy and easily scattered and not so much fun for you to clean up. Nor is it advisable to keep your ferret in an aquarium with the floor covered with cedar chips. Used as a lining for a cage, they will definitely discourage your ferret from using the litter pan because his mess can be easily covered up with them and, consequently, he will have no reason to use a pan. In addition, some ferrets are allergic to cedar, or other wood chips, and will continually sneeze and have watery eyes when such products are used.

If you use a water bowl, make sure that its weight is beyond the lifting capacity of an active, inquisitive kit, who may overturn it with his nose. If your pet or pets habitually play in the water and cause a wet mess in the cage, you might consider using a rabbit or hamster bottle. It can be firmly attached, and the water can be used only for drinking.

LITTER PAN

A litter pan should be tough and durable; it should be made of plastic or metal, which can be repeatedly scoured and handled. The sides of the pan should be about the height of a ferret. If the sides are too high, a young animal will have a difficult and discouraging time on the way to his toilet.

If the sides of the pan aren't high

In many cases, the more time you spend with your ferret, the more it will become attached to you.

enough, your pet will be very likely to back up into the corner of the pan and end up doing his business over the side. Many pet stores that sell ferrets carry especially small litter pans which are ideal for ferrets.

If even a small cat litter pan is too large for the size cage you have chosen, there are many other items that can serve as makeshift ferret-sized litter pans. Such things as a plastic dish pan (if your ferret is young you may want to cut down one of the sides to make it easier for him to get into and out of), a plastic oblong window-box flower planter (metal can be used although it usually leaks and eventually rusts),

and numerous sizes and shapes of plastic food storage containers can all be used quite nicely. I found that the container made to store a one-pound loaf of bread was an especially convenient size for a small cage.

Many readers of my first book have written or called to ask what I used for a litter pan that fit into my shoulder bag (which doubled as Melinda and McGuinn's mobile home). At first I used a plastic container which was five by five by six inches high, and later I used one which was 5½ x 7½ x 4 inches high and designed to hold a quart of ice cream. I found that if I wedged this into the bottom of my shoulder bag

"Many pet stores that sell ferrets carry especially small litter pans which are ideal for ferrets."

If you have two ferrets that are good friends, you may be tempted to bathe them together. This is probably not a good idea, as one wet ferret will be more than a handful, let alone two.

"Before you release your pet ferret to play, the entire room should be closely inspected for holes."

next to a small cardboard box or cardboard bird house that I bought at a pet store, both were held firmly in place and did not tip over. At times I used cat litter in the pan, and at other times I found it was more convenient to use a thick layer of toilet tissue, which was easily disposed of in the nearest ladies room and replaced each time the pan was used.

FERRET-PROOFED ROOMS

Before you release your pet ferret to play, the entire room or rooms should be closely inspected for holes. All openings must be blocked or plastered, especially those around heating ducts and water pipes. My friend Myra Edelstein, who lives in a big apartment building in New York City, found it was very expensive to repair the wall in the apartment of her downstairs neighbor—which it was necessary to tear down in order to retrieve her three-year-old ferret Tara, who disappeared through a hole under the sink and was finally located only because of the tinkling of the bell fastened to her collar.

It's hard to believe, but ferrets can actually squeeze *under* some doors! Check the spacing before you go off and leave your ferret in a room with

Although they will undoubtedly enjoy playing on your bed, pet ferrets should be provided with beds of their own. Pet shops sell various items that can be used as ferret beds.

the door shut, expecting him to stay there—you may find that he can follow you out *after* you shut the door!

Kitchen areas are generally not good play areas for ferrets. Kitchens may contain pipe holes that are accessible only to him. If you allow him in the kitchen, it is wise to first erect a barrier around the bottom of the refrigerator and stove. A ferret will disappear under either appliance to enjoy a long, warm nap. These are not safe locations for a pet. Also,

they are bad areas for a food cache or a toilet. If your ferret finds his way into such a spot, you can try to coax him out with an enticing snack. You can try spraying water in his face. A window cleaner spray bottle that has been cleaned out and filled with clear water works well for this purpose and will encourage most ferrets to vacate an unaccessible location.

If neither method is successful, you may just have to wait until he decides to come out on his own!

"It's hard to believe, but ferrets can actually squeeze under some doors! Check the spacing before you go off and leave your ferret in a room with the door shut, expecting him to stay there—you may find that he can follow you out after you shut the door!"

Ferrets are very inquisitive animals and will investigate just about everything in your home. If you want to keep your ferret safe, you must ferret-proof your home.

Diet
is an important
part of any
animal's life, as
it is
responsible
for his state of
health and his
outlook on life.
The ferret, like
any other
animal, must
have a well-
balanced diet
in order to live
a happy,
healthy life.

FEEDING YOUR FERRET

"To gain the nutritional advantages of many types of food, you can supplement your ferret's basic diet with a variety of other foods."

The bulk of your ferret's diet should be dry. Ferret food, which is specially formulated to meet a ferret's nutritional needs, is available at pet shops. In addition to providing the right nutrients, it also helps to keep a ferret's teeth strong and healthy.

To gain the nutritional advantages of many types of food, you can supplement your ferret's basic diet with a variety of other foods. Canned cat food can be added every few days. You can offer different flavors to vary your pet's diet.

Fish has several outstanding nutritional deficiencies and should be fed no more than once a week, if at all.

In addition to the nutritional advantage of a varied diet, feeding different types of food will, it is hoped, prevent your ferret from becoming a picky eater. Many kits, if fed only one particular brand of chow, will grow up thinking that nothing else, including sirloin steak, is edible and will turn up their noses at anything else you try to feed them. While this is not such a problem when they are young and healthy, it may be literally life-threatening when they are older, should they develop any kind of heart, kidney or liver disease

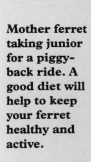

Mother ferret taking junior for a piggy-back ride. A good diet will help to keep your ferret healthy and active.

requiring them to eat a special diet.

Melinda was quite ill with some undiagnosed disease the last two and a half years of her life, and several of the 20 veterinarians I took her to suggested I replace her diet with canned baby foods. Unfortunately, she did not consider these "food" and was unwilling to eat them unless I fed them to her off the end of my finger. Had she been young and healthy, I could and would have merely "starved her out" by continuing to offer them to her with no alternative until she finally got hungry enough to eat them anyway. (Her grandson, Christopher, lost a little weight recently when he didn't eat for three days because he didn't like what I was serving. By the fourth day he was awfully hungry and decided the stuff in his dish *was* better than nothing after all!)

Melinda, however, was too sick to be starved. She was so weak that she literally *would* have starved and died before she became hungry enough to eat. Consequently, every day, three or four times a day for almost a year, I fed her by hand—although she did get so she would eat from a spoon *if* I held the spoon. Any time I fed her the old diet she would eat on her own. After almost a year she seemed no better and no worse than before I changed her diet, and since no one really knew for certain what her problem was, or that changing her diet would ever help, I decided to let her go back to her beloved old diet. During the year she was on soft foods, incidentally, her teeth became quite bad, and at one point she almost died when one of her teeth became infected. Several were so bad that they had to be pulled.

In addition to commercial foods, it is acceptable to offer some table scraps to your pet every few days, and if you wish you may allow him to have some special treats

occasionally, such as small amounts of milk or ice cream.

FRUITS AND VEGETABLES

Ferrets can be given any fruits, vegetables, or meat scraps that they will eat. All ferrets have their own peculiar preferences in food. For example, one ferret I know, Possum Puro, is crazy about blueberries, while her friend Toto has a weakness for tomatoes. Although ferrets have their own preferences in food, you should be careful that they don't become too limited in their definitions of "food." In the end *you* should have the final say about what is or is not food. A young healthy ferret that won't eat fruits or vegetables of *any* kind can often be helped to change his mind by being offered nothing but a variety of fruits and vegetables until his hunger makes them more palatable. Possibly he will develop a taste for them and be more willing to eat them in the future. Since very young kits will eat just about anything, you can usually avoid the "picky eater syndrome" by offering them a variety from the very beginning. Like dogs and cats, however, ferrets should *not* be allowed to have chicken or turkey bones, which splinter easily and can do serious or even fatal damage anywhere along the digestive tract.

A varied diet will help keep ferrets interested in feeding and will also provide more nutrition than a bland, unchanging diet.

"Like dogs and cats . . . ferrets should not *be allowed to have chicken or turkey bones, which splinter easily and can do serious or even fatal damage anywhere along the digestive tract."*

"If you have to supplement a ferret's diet with a dog or cat product, don't forget that a ferret is much smaller. He should accordingly receive a much smaller dose."

MILK AND SWEETS

Most ferrets are fond of milk, but it can cause diarrhea. You should only serve it in small amounts as an infrequent treat. Before serving, it is wise to first dilute the milk with an equal amount of water to help prevent diarrhea.

Generally, you should avoid giving sweets to ferrets. There is little protein or mineral value in candy. If you frequently stray from your pet's normal diet, you can cause sickness. If, however, you cannot resist the joy of giving your ferret a sweet treat, allow him a few licks of ice cream. A tiny portion every few months won't do any harm. You will discover something about your ferret—and most other ferrets: they're wild about ice cream! Once they've been spoiled with a few tastes, you should avoid eating ice cream in front of them, as it will make them very unhappy when you don't share some of it with them— even if it's not good for them!

It is advisable to stay away from all brands of semi-moist cat foods, because they have a very high sugar content (it is used as a preservative) and, in addition, it is very bad for their teeth.

SUPPLEMENTARY DIETS

Since writing the first ferret book, I have learned of numerous ferrets with various undiagnosable illnesses. Several veterinarians I know who specialize in ferrets, including the Bronx Zoo's chief veterinarian, Dr. Emil Dolensek, feel that these illnesses may be related to nutritional deficiencies, so the consensus at this time is that it is advisable to supplement a well-balanced and varied diet with a pet vitamin and mineral product. Care must be taken, however, to prevent an overdose. All pet vitamins and coat conditioners contain vitamin A, one of the fat soluble vitamins which is very toxic in large doses.

One obvious sign of excessive vitamin A is hair loss. If you have to supplement a ferret's diet with a dog or cat product, don't forget that a ferret is much smaller. He should accordingly receive a much smaller dose. If you are confused about dietary supplements and dosages, consult a veterinarian.

Compared to humans, ferrets have an extremely high metabolic rate. Their hearts beat on the average three times per second. Their bodies break down digested food at a rapid pace. They tend to eat small amounts at frequent meals, so it is best to provide nourishment several times a day. For convenience, many pet owners have a dish of dry food available at all times.

Young kits in the midst of fast

Bananas may be the favorite food of one ferret, while others may love apples and oranges. Experiment with your pet to find out what his particular favorites are.

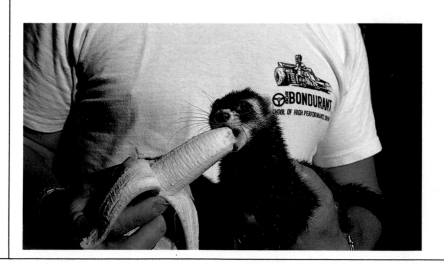

Feeding your pets fruits and vegetables is a wonderful way to add interest to their diet while at the same time adding various nutrients.

Metabolism: the rate at which food is converted into energy by an animal's body.

growth should have a continuous source of dry food available. To provide variety, they may be given several additional portions of canned food daily.

It is not uncommon for kits to eat holes in the towels or linen being used for their bedding. If this happens, there is no reason to panic or run to the vet. The eaten cloth will pass harmlessly through the animal's digestive system. You should prevent this by increasing the amount and/or frequency of feedings, because it is obviously not in the best interest of the long-term health of the pet. Heed the animal's cry for more food by making more available.

When kits approach maturity, their metabolism slows somewhat. Their bodies don't need quite as much nourishment. At this point, all feedings of canned food should be reduced to once a day and, later on, to once every two days.

Make daily observations of the animal's shape. If he begins to put on excess weight, you must stop making dry food available continuously and restrict his feedings to twice a day. If the ferret

does not gain weight after maturity, it is all right to continue the practice of leaving a permanent supply of dry food in his dish. The key to this transition phase in the ferret's life is your observation and understanding. Maintain a diet that keeps the pet trim and active. An overweight ferret, like any other overweight animal, will suffer a host of physical ailments, all leading to a shortened, less active life.

HIDING FOOD

More than once I have been in a restaurant with Melinda and McGuinn hiding in my shoulder bag (also known as their "mobile home") and to keep them quiet and in the bag I have given them little bits of my dinner as they alternately and periodically poked their noses up out of the bag. Later I was quite surprised to find that they had a rather large pile of food in their bed—evidently neither had eaten a thing. I never could figure out what they did with all that time between

getting bites when I thought they were busy eating! All in all, they much preferred the several local restaurants where, instead of having to hide, they were frequent and welcome guests and were given their own chair and served by their friend the waiter or waitress, or sometimes by the owner!

Ferrets, like many other small mammals, "cache" their food. This instinct bolsters the animal's security, knowing that it has a scattered, hidden, and assured food supply. This wild trait carries over into some domestic breeds, one of these being the ferret. Consequently you may find bits of food in their bedding, under furniture, or behind chairs. Ferrets have been known to empty out the entire contents of their bowls and store them in caches. If ferrets don't like what you're serving, it will still give them great pleasure to run off and cache it. Afterward, they'll return for more. Because of the ferret's habit of

It is not a good idea to feed your ferret outdoors, since the potential for escape is so great. It is a good idea, however, to choose a single place for feeding, since this will establish a routine.

hiding leftovers, you should take away moist, perishable food right after mealtime. In this way, you won't have countless forgotten morsels stinking up your home. Dry food is a partial solution or at least an accommodation to this problem. Because it is dehydrated, it will last almost indefinitely, sparing you a foul odor. If a supply of dry food is constantly available, most ferrets (usually as they get older) lose interest or simply become tired of moving it around. If you cannot tolerate an occasional scattering of dry food about the house, you may have to resort to supervised feedings in a selected area. These controlled feedings, could, with the removal of dry food left available continuously, end the problem. Ferret owners should keep in mind that after

several years, many ferrets completely out grow the urge to relocate food.

LIVE FOODS

There is no primitive urge or natural need that requires domestic ferrets to eat mice, birds, frogs, or other small animals, alive or dead. For wild animals, such foods of course would be natural, but they're not for pets. Wild game is usually loaded with parasites that can cause diseases requiring vetcrinary help. Ferrets that have been domestically bred and raised on cat chow will not even recognize small animals as food. Furthermore, a diet of small game will not be an improvement upon the nourishing domestic diet that I have recommended.

"There is no primitive urge or natural need that requires domestic ferrets to eat mice, birds, frogs, or other small animals, alive or dead. For wild animals, such foods of course would be natural, but they're not for pets."

Ferret food, which is available at pet shops, is the basic part of a ferret's diet. It is marketed in variously sized packages to meet the needs of the individual ferret owner. Photo courtesy of Marshall Pet products.

A good diet will add luster and fullness to the ferret's coat and a sparkle to his eyes.

HOUSEBREAKING

Ferrets are creatures of habit. They practice good hygiene and by instinct are similar to cats in their tidiness.

They have a natural tendency to use a corner for a toilet, and to repeatedly use the same corner or corners, and consequently it is fairly easy to train them to use a litter pan.

I find the simplest and easiest way to get a ferret to use a litter pan is to begin by confining him to a very small area. This small area can be a cage, a shower stall with a door your ferret can't push open, or a big cardboard carton. Some people find it convenient to use the bathtub. This has the advantage of being very easy to clean; however, a few of the more agile and persistent kits are eventually able to jump or climb out of it.

CONFINEMENT

In some cases, even the tub or shower stall will be too large an area to use to get your kit started in learning to use the pan, and you'll have to start with something smaller such as a cardboard box or a cage, and move him into the tub or shower later when you are gradually increasing his living area.

In this area of confinement there should be only enough space for a bed, dishes for food and water, a very small place to play, and a litter pan. To discourage him from sleeping in his new litter box, make sure he has a comfortable box or basket he can use as a bed. You can use a cat litter pan, which is available at pet shops; if you can't find one small enough to fit into a cage, a plastic container such as the type used for food storage works well. You can also use a plastic dishpan for this purpose. You should make sure that the height of the pan matches the size of the ferret. You may have to cut off a few inches from the plastic side to give him easier access.

Your kit should remain in this small area all of the time unless you have him out to play and are keeping a close eye on him. You should try to get him to use the pan before he is allowed to come out, and then keep a litter pan nearby and put him in it once every half hour or so to encourage him to use it. Food will go through the entire digestive tract of a ferret in about two hours, and consequently ferrets need to eliminate more frequently than dogs or cats. Your kit will usually have to go to the litter pan shortly after eating or waking from a nap, so at these times you should place him in the pan and keep putting him back in if he tries to get out without using it.

TELL-TALE BEHAVIOR

If you watch your pet carefully, you will learn to recognize the behavior that indicates that it's time to use the pan again. Your ferret will more than likely become restless, possibly even running around in circles, and then back up a few steps while lifting his tail. If you do catch him in the act of starting to go to the toilet elsewhere, immediately pick him up and put him into the pan.

While you are holding your ferret he will probably struggle to get down if he needs to eliminate. At these times he will usually put up more of a fight and be more insistent about being put down than he would if he wanted to be set free for any other reason, because, fortunately for you, most ferrets will do all they

"Ferrets are creatures of habit. They practice good hygiene and by instinct are similar to cats in their tidiness."

In the past, due to the ferret's musk and urine odors, many pets, especially males, were kept in outdoor cages. With the accessibility of descenting and neutering operations, however, the pet ferret has now taken his place inside the home.

"If you keep the litter pan too clean, your ferret will use it for a play area. He will enjoy digging, rooting, and scattering litter."

Mature children may be taught the proper way to maintain a ferret's cage, but younger children are best left out of this activity. It is a good idea to supervise the interaction between children and ferrets.

can to avoid urinating while you are holding them.

PAN-TRAINING

Start the pan-training procedure by placing a piece of newspaper in the bottom of the pan and smearing it rather generously in each of the corners and around the sides with some of your kit's feces. Be sure to use a sufficient amount of feces to discourage your kit from taking the newspaper out and tearing it into little pieces, which many kits will do to entertain themselves if the paper is clean enough. Making the pan dirty will make an undesirable place to play as well as encouraging your kit to use it for a toilet. Considering the alternatives of messing in their food, play area or bed, most ferrets will readily choose to use the pan.

Once the newspaper in the pan gets wet with urine, sprinkle a thin layer of cat litter on top of it. This should take as little as five or six tablespoons of litter. Regular clay litter can be used for this purpose; however, I prefer to use the green litter which is in the form of small pellets and can be purchased in almost any pet store. I find that this does not stick to little ferret paws and track outside the pan quite as much as the conventional clay litter

does. In addition, the alfalfa in the green litter helps to control the urine odor. Most people, incidentally, find that ferret urine does not have nearly as strong a smell as cat urine. Although green litter is more expensive than clay litter, I find that rabbit chow, which is also made from alfalfa, makes a good substitute and is appreciably cheaper—and neither my cats nor ferrets can seem to tell the difference!

As the litter becomes soaked with urine, add another layer of fresh litter to the top of the wet litter. Continue to do this until the pan becomes about one-fourth to one-half filled with litter. The idea is to keep the litter on the top clean and somewhat dry so that your kit won't get his feet wet when he uses the pan, while at the same time allowing it to remain rather dirty underneath the top layer so that if your kit begins to dig in the pan he will quickly uncover a mess. While ferrets love to dig, even the most playful kit usually will avoid digging in a dirty litter pan.

If you keep the litter pan too clean, your ferret will use it for a play area. He will enjoy digging, rooting, and scattering litter. He will create a mess that you might never have imagined possible for

such a small critter. The good time, of course, will be on you, because you will have to clean it up. In addition, you will have a pet harboring twisted ideas about where the toilet is. If the litter pan is clean, for example, he may choose his bed or play area for a toilet and end up sleeping in the would-be litterpan. (He wouldn't dare dirty such a nice, clean sandbox!)

CLEANING UP

The effort to keep the litter pan slightly littered must be complemented by an effort to maintain a spotlessly clean cage. This will keep you on your toes for the first few days. You should clean it several times a day, because the pet, in the middle of toilet training, may leave droppings outside the litter pan. Eventually, he will get the message. It is recommended that you apply a deodorizing disinfectant when cleaning. This will help to erase any odors of urine or droppings. The strong smell of the disinfectant will discourage some ferrets from using the area for a toilet again. In two or three days' time, this constant reinforcement of the pan as the sole toilet area usually creates a habit. The ferret will then incorporate it into his cage-life routine. During future cleaning, do not completely replace the soiled litter with a fresh amount. It is best

to leave a small portion of the litter containing some droppings. This will continue to reinforce the pan as the toilet area. As the months go by and the ferret gains maturity, less and less soiled litter need be left in the pan. After a period of three months, you will be able to replace the complete amount of soiled litter during cleaning. Your ferret should be well beyond any urge to play in it. If, however, the kit has not learned his toilet lessons, you will have to continue the partial cleaning procedure. At six to seven months, the ferret will mature and become an adult. Hopefully, you will be able to keep the pan totally clean by this time.

You may encounter another difficulty concerning the litterpan. This will be the result of the ferret's natural drive to frequently move things around and rearrange his living space. Sometimes, during a supreme effort to move the litterpan, he may up-end it. This, of course, will put an instant halt to all pan-training efforts. To remedy this problem, or better yet to prevent it, you should figure out a way to keep the litter pan in place by tying it or weighting it down.

In an effort to channel these busy moving energies into more desirable activities, you might give him some dog or cat toys. These will keep him occupied, and his mind will no

"The effort to keep the litter pan slightly littered must be complemented by an effort to maintain a spotlessly clean cage."

"Although plentiful and inexpensive, newspaper can become an entertaining novelty in the routine of cage life. The kits may delight in tearing it up and spreading it all around."

longer be so intent on redecorating the cage. Make sure you give him a toy that is tough and safe. These playful novelties should be changed or rotated frequently to keep your ferret from becoming bored with them.

NEWSPAPER VS LITTER

It generally takes very little or no effort on your part to get a ferret to use a litter pan if you keep him confined and add the litter gradually. Some people prefer to not use litter at all, but instead continue to use newspaper in the bottom of the pan. This is a reasonable alternative, but generally less desirable because the kit frequently cannot avoid getting his feet wet, thus contributing to the odor problem, and also because the newspaper must be changed more often than litter. Paper towels can be substituted for newspaper. They have the advantage of being slightly more absorbent, but they also are considerably more expensive.

You may decide to spread newspaper in the litter pan. Although plentiful and inexpensive, newspaper can become an entertaining novelty in the routine of cage life. The kits may delight in tearing it up and spreading it all around. One solution is to leave the paper in a dirty, foul condition to deter the fun and games. If you don't like that idea, try wetting the newspaper slightly. Water will sometimes deter ferret activity. You will probably have to clean it more often, because wet paper won't absorb as much.

It is extremely rare that a ferret, when caged or confined to a small area, will not use his pan, and when he won't it is usually under unusual circumstances. For example, on more than one occasion I have taken care of someone's ferret while they were on vacation and found that even though the animals were kept in fairly small cages, they used both the bed and the litter pan for a toilet and consequently ended up sleeping

A ferret that is properly housebroken will be a happy ferret that can be given ample opportunity to explore his surroundings.

in their own mess and getting very dirty. At the same time they also had a decreased appetite, lost a great deal of weight, and appeared markedly depressed and apathetic. Evidently these animals were sensitive to and upset by the change in environment and daily routine, because when their owners took them home they immediately resumed using the pan and gradually gained back the weight they had lost. Most ferrets, incidentally, are not the least bit upset by being away from home and can be boarded with no problem whatsoever.

TOILET PROBLEMS

Getting a ferret to use the litter pan while confined to a cage or small area is definitely the easy part. Getting him to go *back* to the pan when he has free run of the house is a more difficult project and requires patience, effort, and sometimes considerable tolerance on your part. Ferrets are not cats, and they show more variability from animal to animal than cats do in their toilet habits. Almost all cats will use the litter pan 100% of the time, provided that the pan is not too dirty and they are not unduly upset. Some ferrets will use the pan 100% of the time like cats do, and then again some ferrets won't. Some ferrets will use the pan most of the time, and most

ferrets will use the pan some of the time. Rarely, at the other extreme, a few ferrets won't use the pan very much of the time. How good they are about using the pan depends a lot on their own inherent tendencies and to some extent on your diligence in guiding and encouraging them. If you are expecting a cat-like creature or if you are the kind of person who would get upset about an occasional "accident" then a ferret is not the pet for you! Most ferret owners find that ferrets have so many other good qualities that they are well worth the little trouble that they cause.

Once the habit of using the litter pan is firmly established, usually after a month or two, you can begin to try to get your ferret to use the pan when he is not confined to a small area. This is most easily done by increasing his living area gradually. Put his cage in a small room with the cage door left open, or put his bed and litter pan in a small room such as the bathroom. Once again make sure that he uses the pan before you allow him to come out and play, and place him in the pan at regular intervals while he is out of his cage.

If he doesn't use the litter pan when he is in a small room, then put him into an even smaller area, such as the bathtub or shower stall. You may find that you have to put him

"Oddly enough, for some unknown reason, when there are two pans in one large room, some ferrets will run back and forth, hopping into and out of one pan and then the other for several times before deciding upon which one to use!"

back in his cage or the original area of confinement. Leave him there for several days and then try a slightly larger area again.

When your ferret is consistently using his litter pan in a small room, then you can increase the space in which he is allowed to run free by adding another room. When you do this you will more than likely need to put an additional litter pan in the new room. Many ferrets will use the litter pan when it is nearby, but some will not bother to travel any great distance to get to one, and they are more likely to use the pan when there is one available in each room. Oddly enough, for some unknown reason, when there are two pans in one large room, some ferrets will run back and forth, hopping into and out of one pan and then the other for several times before deciding upon which one to use!

Keep increasing your ferret's area one room at a time until you have included all the rooms in which he will be allowed to roam free, decreasing the area when necessary to get him to use the pan. If he does have an accident somewhere, be sure to clean it up thoroughly, so that no odor is left to encourage him to use that spot again.

URINE ODORS

Unfortunately, although the odor of urine will invite a ferret to use the same spot again, other odors don't seem to *discourage* him from using a particular spot. I know of people who have applied such strong smelling things as ammonia, chlorine bleach, vinegar, and pepper to an inconvenient corner their ferret had chosen for a toilet in the hope that this treatment would make the area unacceptable and force the pet to pick out another corner. Thus far I know of no one who has had any success in finding a substance which acts as a deterrent—including any of the various dog and cat repellents sold at pet stores.

I do know of two older ferrets, Possum and Toto, who both faithfully use their litter pans 100% of the time for several months in a row, and then all of a sudden one day, for no apparent reason, they stop using their pans. When this was discovered by their owner, they got locked up in their cage for a few days. When they are again allowed out they are very good about using their pans for another two or three months before becoming recidivists, at which time their brief "jailing" is repeated with the same results.

A young ferret will often get the right idea about using the litter pan by watching an older, properly housebroken companion.

A demonstration of the proper way to hold a ferret.

There are several alternative methods for pan-training your ferret when he is not caged, one of which is to wait and see which corner or corners your ferret prefers to use for a toilet, and then to put his pan or pans in the place or places that he has chosen. Or, you may wish to forego the pan altogether and just use newspaper, especially if he's chosen a place so small that you can't fit a pan into it. This is something akin to letting your ferret teach *you* to put clean paper where he wants to go. Although this is somewhat less desirable than your teaching *him* where to go, it is, on occasion, the most practical and realistic approach. I know many ferrets who have free run of very large houses who have trained their owners in this manner. They have five or six spots throughout the entire house where their owners dutifully keep clean newspapers for them. They never soil in any other place.

Sometimes ferrets may soil the wall in the course of using the newspaper. The best solution is a preventive one: tape some newspaper several inches up on the wall.

CAGE TRAINING

Another reasonable alternative for the ferret who is inconsistent about using the pan is to make him live in a cage except when you have him out to play and can keep an eye on his activities. This will definitely be less trouble for you, and although it is somewhat less than ideal for your ferret, it is preferable to abandoning him because he is inconsistent in his toilet habits. I know many ferrets who live quite happily in a cage, being let out once or twice a day to play.

One reader of my last book, Merry

"I know many ferrets who live quite happily in a cage, being let out once or twice a day to play."

"Some ferret owners find that it is helpful to give their pet a reward consisting of a small bite or two of their favorite food every time they see him use the litter pan."

Kahn of Maquoketa, Iowa, wrote me about her experience in trying to pan train her two ferrets, Sunshine and Piccolo: "It seems that they know they are supposed to use the litter box for their 'business', however, they do not seem to realize that they aren't supposed to go elsewhere to relieve themselves. Every so often they will decide the same old litter box in the same old corner is boring, and will try a new area. At first we placed litter boxes in every corner that seemed to appeal to them. Maintenance of so many boxes was not only ridiculous, but also did not solve the problem. Now we watch the ferrets very closely. Whenever they back into the wrong corner (raising their tail in a bathroom 'salute'), my husband or I will shout *'NO!'* and hustle them over to the litter box. This usually works, although Piccolo is sometimes obstinate and will run back to the wrong corner and try again. We have repeated the process until she finally gives up and goes in the litter box. Sunshine is better than Piccolo, but even she will try a new territory every so often, and consequently we keep them caged except for about an hour, both in the morning and again in the evening, during which times we supervise them closely."

Some ferrets have the peculiar habit of going right *next* to their litter pan rather than *in* it. Sometimes this may be because the litter is too dirty. When the pan is cleaned out more often they will use it as they should. In other instances, however, they will go next to the pan for no apparent reason. In these cases it is advisable to put newspaper down under the pan and in the area around the pan—and then you can just be grateful when they hit the paper!

REWARD VS PUNISHMENT

I have found that such things as rubbing their noses in their mess when they relieve themselves in the wrong place, or spanking them as some people suggest, is generally ineffective. Ferrets don't seem to be too impressed by such punishment and tend to respond much better to reward for using the right place. Some ferret owners find that it is helpful to give their pet a reward consisting of a small bite or two of their favorite food every time they see him use the litter pan. This, of course, means watching the animal closely so that the reward can be given immediately after he steps out of the pan. In order to make the reward a reinforcement for the

Small litter pans for cats may be used inside or outside the ferret's cage. If they are used inside, be sure they do not take up too much room.

desired behavior, the ferret must be able to connect the reward with using the pan.

I also know of numerous ferrets who are kept caged part of the time. They have learned that they have to use the pan before they are allowed to come out of the cage in the morning. Consequently, whenever they are put back into the cage before they are ready to go to sleep, they will quickly jump into their pan and use it or lift their tail and go

FERRET INTELLIGENCE

Their small size should not deceive anyone into thinking that ferrets are not intelligent animals. With time and proper training, they will know that the litter pan is there for its one and only use.

Occasionally, some ferrets know but apparently just don't care. When caught in the act of preparing to go in the wrong place, they will stop and run over to the pan and use it as they should—but only if they are

"Their small size should not deceive anyone into thinking that ferrets are not intelligent animals."

A housebroken ferret can become an important member of any household, just like a dog or cat.

through the motions of using it. Then they wait expectantly at the door to be let back out. Many of these same ferrets will also voluntarily return to their cage, which is left open so that they may come and go as they please, when they want to eat, sleep, or use the litter pan. Both Melinda and McGuinn have been known to crawl up onto the sides and top of their cage in an attempt to get back in to go to sleep when I have forgotten to leave one of the doors open for them. Unfortunately, they have never crawled on their cage to get in to use the pan, which doesn't seem to be as important to them as their bed!

caught and scolded.

Some ferrets are so well trained that when no pan is available they will use anything that resembles a pan. Once when we were visiting friends, McGuinn used a shoe box (complete with shoes!) for a litter pan, it being the closest thing to a pan that she could find at the time!

Both Melinda and Moseley usually seem to be able to locate and are quite willing to use the cat pan when we visit friends who have cats. Sometimes the cats aren't too happy about that!

Melinda is very good about using the little litter pan that I carry for her in my shoulder bag. She is so good, in fact, that one night several

Some ferrets enjoy walking around outdoors, but many prefer to be carried.

"Whenever I have baby ferrets in the house . . . she [Melinda] stops using the pan and instead uses the floor in front of their cages."

Ferrets, like most dogs, cats, children, and adults, usually won't hesitate to tell you what they want.

years ago when I had her out with me, someone else was holding her and she needed to use the pan. She couldn't find my bag, so she jumped into the handbag belonging to the girl who was holding her and used that instead. It was the best she could do under the circumstances; fortunately, the owner of the bag was a good friend of hers!

On the other hand, there are times when Melinda is especially bad about using the litter pan. Whenever I have baby ferrets in the house for descenting, or older ferrets for boarding, she stops using the pan and instead uses the floor in front of their cages. I assume that she is making some kind of a territorial claim by such behavior, although none of my other ferrets do this.

Once Melinda and I were spending the night at the home of a friend, Margaret Hooper, who also has three ferrets. Early in the evening Melinda made her statement by defecating in front of the ferret cage in the kitchen. Later, in the middle of the night, she got out of bed where she

was sleeping with me and dutifully used the litter pan right next to the bed—presumably because she was too sleepy to go all the way to the kitchen.

SPITE WORK

McGuinn also used to soil in the middle of the floor, but it was to make a different kind of statement. For example, one afternoon we were visiting my friend Larry Goldblatt, who insisted that I allow McGuinn to run around the living room. My ferrets aren't usually allowed to roam free in other people's houses, because of the absence of litter pans and also because most of these houses are not "ferret-proofed" and I'm afraid they will find and disappear down some formerly unnoticed hole. I got McGuinn out of Larry's large potted plant twice and scolded her each time, but she was determined to do some hole digging and got back in a third time. I took her out and spanked her, and

This ferret is sleeping while his young owner watches television. It is most important to put your ferret into his litter pan when he first wakes up, because this is one of the times that he will most certainly need to use it.

". . . look on the bright side—your ferret would certainly be more trouble (and make a lot more mess) if he weighed 90 or 100 pounds."

as soon as I put her down she ran right to the middle of the floor and defecated. I'm not sure whether she did it simply because she was upset or whether she did it to punish *me* for punishing her. I do know that she is aware of the fact that I want her to use the litter pan, because she will jump in the pan and use it when I catch her starting to soil on the paper next to the pan and yell at her, *"McGuinn, use the pan!"*

Of all the calls and letters I get from ferret owners asking for advice or information, probably at least one-third of them are from people who haven't been able to get their ferrets 100% pan-trained. They want to know what they can do about it.

What *do* you do when you've tried everything and you just can't get your free-roaming ferret to use the litter pan on a regular basis? You can either keep him in a cage or else keep him in a room with a "wash and walk" floor and clean it up when he goes in the wrong place. He's probably worth it! And you can always just look on the bright side— your ferret would certainly be more trouble (and make a lot more mess) if he weighed 90 or 100 pounds.

FERRET GROOMING

Ferrets are naturally clean animals and bathing is not a necessity; however, an occasional bath, assuming your pet is descented and altered, will help keep your pet odor-free. If you take your ferret out with you to meet people, you may want to bathe him as frequently as once every five or six days, as some people think animals should have absolutely *no* smell at all. This is a somewhat unreasonable expectation. You should be able to bathe your ferret that often without drying out his skin, but this will depend on the season (the skin tends to dry out more in the winter when the humidity is low) and the individual animal. You can safely begin bathing your kit as soon as he is six or seven weeks old, as long as you take the usual precautions to keep him from getting chilled. In addition to reducing odor, a bath will make your ferret's coat look fluffy and full.

While most ferrets are not particularly enthusiastic about getting a bath, they quickly learn to tolerate it without a struggle, especially if it is a frequent, regular event. A few ferrets actually seem to learn to enjoy it.

Jerry and Robynn Huffman of Independence, Missouri, say that while their three ferrets still don't look forward to the "weekly weasel washes" with eager anticipation, "they always submit without any struggle as we go through the routine of 'the catch', 'the capture', 'the crazy foamy stuff in the kitchen sink', 'the drying', and then (the best part), the 'ferret, rabid-dog look

alike contest', which is only momentary craziness, and always the inevitable product of a bath."

Melinda and McGuinn thoroughly enjoy a good baby shampoo. They eat it up like whipped cream, including the lather which they lick from themselves and my hands. Most ferrets will also try to eat soap, which is generally harmless but certainly not recommended.

I have learned from experience that bath time can quickly turn into an animal versus human free-for-all. For best results, first ensure that the bath area is warm and free of drafts to prevent your pet from getting a chill and catching a cold. Run the tap water until it is lukewarm. Hold the ferret under the faucet or spray attachment. After a thorough soaking, apply a "tear-free" pet shampoo or baby shampoo to his upper back. Lather him gently from head to tail. Make sure you thoroughly lather the face and head, as this is where most of the musk odor seems to concentrate. Don't be concerned about stinging his eyes. The tear-free shampoo is perfectly painless; it's designed for this type of application. If you suspect that your ferret has fleas, use a flea shampoo designed for cats. Simply follow the instructions on the label. This flea shampoo, while effective, should not be used on a frequent basis.

THE RINSE

When you have performed a complete shampoo lathering of the pet, hold him under the faucet or sprayer in the same way as in the initial soaking. Rinse him as you would rinse shampoo from your own hair. Exercise care when rinsing his face to prevent the pain and trauma of getting water into his nose. After rinsing, allow him to drip briefly to shed excess water. Ferrets work hard to dry themselves. All you have to do is lay an unfolded towel next to

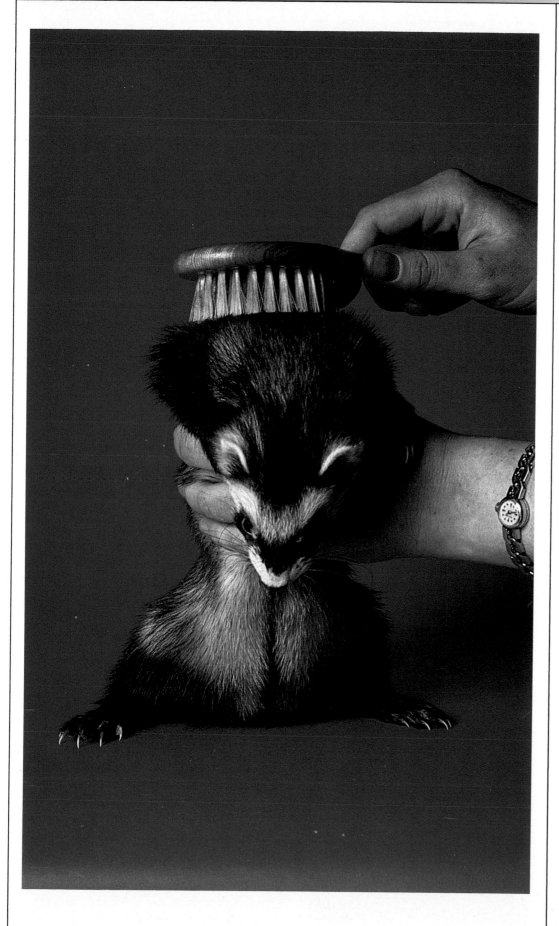

Most ferrets will not tolerate brushing; in fact, brushing is not a necessity for pet ferrets. The preferred method of removing dead hair from the coat during the shedding period is plucking.

Most ferrets do not like being bathed, but they will usually learn to tolerate it.

Begin the bath by soaking the ferret in lukewarm water.

Lather the ferret from head to tail with a mild, tear-free pet or baby shampoo.

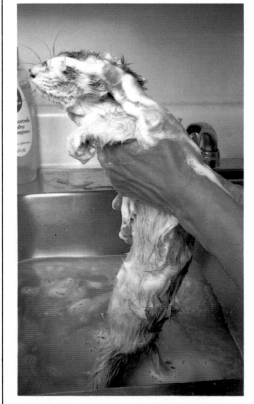

him and he will burrow and rub himself against it. Unless your house is immaculate and you don't mind damp spots, don't let him loose. His instinct will be to rub and roll against any convenient surface to get dry. In doing so, he may end up accumulating more dirt than when you started. The best place for towel drying is either the drained bathtub or sink, or his bed or yours. Just give him a towel and watch him frolic. You will observe that after a

bath most ferrets become intensely frisky and playful.

DRYING

I know of a few ferrets that will allow their owners to dry them with a hair dryer, but mine truly hated it and put up such a struggle on the two occasions I tried it that I quickly abandoned the idea. If you do use a hair dryer on your ferret, make sure that it is on a "warm" rather than a "hot" setting, which will burn your pet's skin. It is also advisable to keep testing the temperature on the back of your hand, as many dryers get hotter after they have been on for a while.

SWIMMING

Like McGuinn, most ferrets do not voluntarily take to the water; rather, they must be gently placed in it. After they are in the water, however, some of them appear to be having a good time. If your pet is one who seems to enjoy bathing, you might allow him more time in the water. Let him take a semi-swim; fill the sink or bathtub with only about three to five inches of warm water so he can touch bottom. If he can touch, he will not be so intent on survival and will be more relaxed.

Ferrets are natural swimmers, although they usually prefer to bypass water. The vast majority swim only to get to the nearest shore to avoid drowning. There are, however, rare cases of ferrets who swim voluntarily, even in deep water.

Dusti Truran claims that in the summer when it was hot, her two ferrets, Maybelle and Farrah, used to voluntarily go into her swimming pool and swim about for a while, but she never could decide if they did it because they liked the swimming or did it merely to cool off.

Melinda and McGuinn have been swimming several times in both pools and at Malibu Beach. They unequivocally *hated* it, but understandably seemed to hate the ocean more than the pools. They did enjoy digging holes in the sand if they had somewhere to go to get out of the sun and into the shade!

A SHOWER

Another alternative for bathing your ferret is the shower. I know of several ferret owners who find that the most convenient way to give

You can purchase grooming products that are specially formulated for ferrets. Photo courtesy of Four Paws.

"Ferrets are natural swimmers, although they usually prefer to bypass water. The vast majority swim only to get to the nearest shore to avoid drowning."

Be sure to dry your ferret thoroughly (or be sure he dries himself thoroughly!).

Some ferrets will be more cooperative than others when it comes to having their claws clipped. It is a good idea to have a special treat with which to distract your pet during this operation. Some owners try to clip a few claws while their pets are asleep. In addition, most owners recommend using human type nail clippers rather than the type used for dogs.

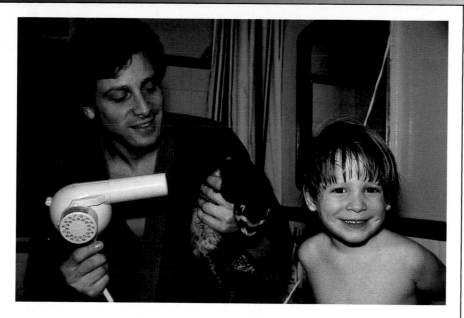

If your ferret will permit it, you may wish to use a blow dryer on his coat. If you do, be sure that the setting is not too hot for your ferret.

their pet a bath is to take him into the shower with them, soap him up, rinse him off, and turn him loose out on the bathroom floor with several towels to dry himself off.

Some ferrets even *like* the shower. Sandie Foster's ferret, Thomas, loved the shower and if given the chance would climb in with her and stay until she finished. The only problem with this was that, in addition to enjoying the shower, he also thought it was great fun to nip at Sandie's toes and make her yell. Naturally this made him an unpopular shower mate, so he usually got locked out of the bathroom when Sandie showered (if she merely threw him out of the shower he'd keep coming back) and he had to take his own weekly shower alone! Not only did Thomas love little showers, but he also loved big showers, and one of his favorite pastimes was to go for a walk in the rain!

BRUSHING

Ferrets have wash-and-wear coats that rarely need brushing or combing—in fact, most ferrets hate to be brushed and will not sit still for it. Unlike dogs and cats, who are continually shedding dead hair all year 'round, ferrets shed only at the

time of their coat change, usually twice a year. While frequent brushing of a dog or cat helps remove the dead hair and reduces the amount of fur available to be left behind on furniture and carpeting, it does not serve this purpose in ferrets unless the ferret happens to be in the middle of a coat change. Since the ferret loses all its dead hair at about the same time, usually over a period of several weeks, its period of

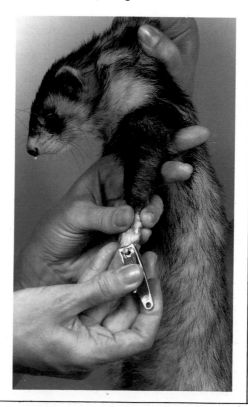

"Ferrets have wash-and-wear coats that rarely need brushing or combing—in fact, most ferrets hate to be brushed and will not sit still for it."

Most ferrets hate having their claws clipped. Having a second person to assist you during this procedure will make the job much easier.

shedding is more intense than that of a dog or cat when it comes to leaving fur all over the house. Brushing helps reduce this extensive shedding; however, I have found brushing to be much less effective than "plucking."

PLUCKING

To pluck my ferrets I wait until they start shedding enough to leave a furry mess behind them wherever they go, and then I just hold them over a waste basket and pluck out all of their dead fur—using much the same technique as one uses in plucking a chicken—except that I do not soak them in boiling water first! Admittedly they did look a little strange when I finished, because they were instantly transformed from fluffy longhaired creatures to almost bald, skinny looking oddities, having no fur left to speak of except for the very beginnings of a new coat, which was sometimes as little as an eighth of an inch long. I found it preferable to have their fur all together in the waste basket rather than scattered in clumps all over the house. Since the dead hair falls out quite readily, this plucking procedure is totally painless. All of my ferrets were amazingly cooperative in my endeavor to rid them of it and never put up even the least bit of a struggle. They clearly preferred being plucked to being brushed!

Occasionally a ferret will do a little grooming on his own, much like a cat does. McGuinn frequently washes her feet, and all of my ferrets will wash their face once in a while.

THE EARS

Like other animals, ferrets can develop a build up of wax in their ears, so you may wish to clean them out occasionally, using a cotton-tipped swab. Most ferrets hate to have their ears cleaned even more than they hate having their nails trimmed, so getting an assistant to help hold your pet while you work is highly recommended. You can avoid puncturing the eardrum if you keep the swab pointed in a direction parallel to, rather than perpendicular to, your pet's head while you clean out his ears. The technique for cleaning a ferret's ears is basically the same as that used for cleaning a dog's or cat's ears, but if you are uncertain about it, you can have your veterinarian show you how to do it properly.

CLAWS

Ferrets have thin, tiny claws. When they grow long, their edges feel sharp and scratchy. Excessive claw length will eventually lead to snagging on bedspreads, curtains, or sofas. For this reason, the claws should be kept short with frequent trimmings.

Claw trimming is best accomplished with regular human nail clippers that most people are used to. Trace the ferret's claw back until you come to a vein. It is best to cut the claw right in front of the vein. This will insure the shortest cut. Be careful not to cut too close. If you accidentally cut the vein, your pet will bleed and will be most uncooperative during future claw trimmings. If you are confused or faint-hearted about trimming claws, a live demonstration by a veterinarian will help.

You will find that ferrets do not enjoy having their claws trimmed. They will express this dislike by squirming, rolling, and trying to free themselves from your grasp. It is therefore best to have someone hold the animal while you do the clipping.

There is yet another sneaky but creative method of claw trimming when no assistance is available. Tiptoe in and gingerly start clipping

Claws that have grown too long will snag and can possibly rip curtains, blankets, etc. Be sure to clip your pet's claws regularly.

"Sometimes it helps to distract your ferret with a special treat, and if you have the person who is holding him give him a pat of butter or a lick of ice cream, he may be willing to ignore the manicure you're giving him."

while the pet sleeps. My success rate is anywhere from one to three claws before waking them.

One good way to hold your ferret is to grasp him by the scruff of the neck in the same manner as a mother cat (or mother ferret for that matter!) carries her kittens. This will immobilize any ferret considerably; however, most are still capable of putting up quite a struggle when you begin to trim their nails.

Sometimes it helps to distract your ferret with a special treat, and if you have the person who is holding him give him a pat of butter or a lick of ice cream, he may be willing to ignore the manicure you're giving him. Melinda hated having her nails trimmed but oddly enough loved to kiss and was very easily distracted with kisses, which were usually enough to draw her attention away from her feet so that I could clip all twenty toenails without any opposition on her part!

FERRET HEALTH

Distemper: a highly contagious viral disease marked by fever and by respiratory and nervous system symptoms.

Unlike many exotic pets, which are susceptible to a variety of strange and exotic diseases and are consequently difficult to maintain in a state of good health, ferrets are basically hardy animals. If the necessary immunizations are kept up to date and they are given a balanced diet, you should expect to have no more health problems with your ferret than you do with the average dog or cat.

Ferrets are extremely susceptible to canine distemper, which is invariably fatal to them. For this reason they should be vaccinated regularly against this disease using modified live virus canine distemper vaccine. Products of any origin except ferret may be used; however, high passage chick embryo vaccines are felt by some authorities (including Dr. Emil Dolensek, Chief Veterinarian of the Bronx Zoo) to be the safest with the least chance of causing a reaction. Killed distemper vaccines should not be used because they have been found to be ineffective in a few ferrets and, in addition, the immunity they provide does not last as long as that of live or modified live virus vaccines. Vaccine prepared from ferret cell culture should never be used because the attenuated virus may retain its virulence for its natural host. As a consequence, it can cause distemper in your ferret rather than prevent it.

The first vaccination against canine distemper should be given when your ferret is six to eight weeks old. Booster shots should be given twice, at intervals of two to three weeks following the initial inoculation.

A mother who has been vaccinated for distemper passes along a temporary natural immunity to her offspring *in utero* and also in her breast milk, especially during the first 24 hours of life. Kits should receive their first vaccination at six to eight weeks of age. Otherwise, as immunity from the mother begins to wear off, the kits will be left unprotected against distemper.

Studies of mink kits show that maternally acquired immunity can last for as long as 12 weeks. Since any vaccination given to the kits while this temporary immunity is still active is not effective in protecting them against distemper, it is important that the last booster be given after 12 weeks of age when all of their temporary immunity is gone.

Your ferret, like a dog, should receive a yearly canine distemper shot along with a routine check-up.

Ferrets are susceptible to infection with *Leptospira* bacteria, and some veterinarians recommend vaccination using vaccine against the canine strains.

Canine hepatitis is not thought to cause clinical infection in ferrets. This immunization may be given without harm, however, so that vaccination against canine distemper can generally be done safely using a 3-in-1 product which includes distemper, hepatitis, and leptospirosis vaccines.

Although it has been the subject of continuing controversy in the past, recent studies (done by Dr. John Gorham at Washington State University and Dr. Colin Parrish at Cornell University) in which ferrets were challenged with feline distemper virus as well as canine parvovirus have shown that ferrets are not susceptible to either of these diseases and consequently do not need to be inoculated against them.

A healthy ferret will have a beautiful coat and bright shining eyes. On the whole, most ferrets are hardy animals.

Murine: relating to certain species of rats and mice, especially the common household mouse.

Adrenal cortical carcinoma in a ferret.

RABIES

While ferrets are susceptible to rabies, it is highly unlikely that your pet ferret, kept indoors and not allowed out of doors without supervision, will come into contact with any animal with rabies. Consequently, it is highly unlikely that it will contract this disease. *Veterinary Public Health Notes,* prepared by the Bureau of Epidemiology, Center for Disease Control in Atlanta, Georgia, in October 1980, has this to say about ferrets and rabies: "Although studies on susceptibility of ferrets to rabies have been reported, as a mustelid the ferret is assumed to be highly susceptible and capable of transmitting rabies if infected. Two cases of ferret rabies have been reported in the United States, 1 in 1954 and 1 in 1978. No data are available on the first case; the second case was in a pet for which an exposure could not be determined, although there was a recognized possibility that the animal might have received live rabies vaccine.

"It appears that the ferret, while a potential source of rabies exposure for man, is much less likely to be exposed to rabies that are pet skunks, raccoons or foxes, which are often trapped in the wild and then sold as pets. If, in the investigation of a ferret bite, the investigator can be reasonably assured that the animal has had no contact with indigenous rabies vectors and was not vaccinated with MLV (modified live virus) rabies vaccine, then the likelihood of the ferret's having rabies seems extremely remote, and antirabies treatment of the bite victim would not seem warranted. If, on the other hand, the ferret has possibly been in contact with wildlife, then rabies should be considered."

Because rabies is a fatal disease easily transmitted from the saliva of an infected animal to man through a break in the skin or mucous membranes, whether through a bite wound or through a pre-existing cut or abrasion, it is a good idea to vaccinate your ferret yearly against this disease. The greatest value of this inoculation (except in rare areas or under unusual circumstances where your pet may come into contact with a rabid animal) is that it will allow you to reassure anyone bitten by your pet that he or she is not in danger of contracting rabies. If your ferret has been vaccinated with killed tissue rabies vaccine and you can prove it, it may save the person bitten from having to have rabies prophylaxis, a series of painful injections, as well as possibly saving your ferret from being sacrificed so that his brain tissue can be analyzed for the presence of rabies virus. Fortunately, in recent years more and more pet-quality ferrets are being sold. These animals are bred for good temperaments and rarely bite, thus helping to prevent problems from occurring in the first place!

Ferrets should be vaccinated against rabies with killed tissue rabies vaccine of murine origin. This is extremely important, as live or modified live virus can give your ferret rabies. Vaccination can be done at three months of age, and boosters should be administered yearly, again taking care that only

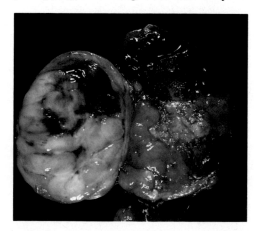

Before purchasing your pet, it may be a good idea to ask the seller to recommend a vet who is familiar with ferrets.

killed tissue vaccine is used.

It should be noted that at the present time there are no vaccines or other drugs on the market which have been tested and approved by the Federal Food and Drug Administration for use in ferrets. This situation will no doubt change as ferrets become even more popular and the number of ferret owners continues to increase.

PARASITES

Not surprisingly, ferrets are susceptible to fleas (*Ctenocephalides* spp). You can check for fleas by gently blowing on your pet, which will part the fur and enable you to see the skin where fleas may be crawling around. Little speckles of black "dirt" on the base of the hair near the skin may also be a sign of fleas. Flea bites will cause your ferret to scratch himself. However, ferrets tend to scratch themselves frequently, and this alone should not be taken as a sign that they have fleas. If your ferret has been in a flea infested area or around other animals that have fleas, he is quite likely to have these parasites, but you should be certain that he really does before treating him, as it is best to avoid unnecessary exposure to pesticides. When you are in doubt, you should consult a veterinarian.

If your ferret has fleas, a spray or powder containing pyrethrins, carbanyl 1 malathione 1%, or rotenone can be applied. Be sure that all flea medications used are safe for cats—some insecticides for dogs may be toxic to ferrets. In difficult cases where powders or sprays are not effective, it may be necessary to use a flea bomb in the areas of your house where your ferret roams, in addition to having your veterinarian give your pet a flea dip.

Frequent scratching, especially around the head and ears, can be a sign of ear mites. These parasites (*Otodectes cynotis*) will cause your pet's ears to look dirty but should not be confused with the normal reddish wax that is secreted by the ferret's ears. If mites are present your veterinarian will be able to see them. This condition can be treated with prolonged application of mild feline miticides such as rotenone or pyrethrin products.

Ear mites should always be treated as soon as they are discovered; left untreated they can cause ear infections which can sometimes progress to deafness.

Sarcoptic mange (scabies) can also cause scratching in ferrets and can be treated with ivernectin or lime sulphur dips. While not common, ringworm (*Trichophyton mentagrophytes* and *Microsporum canis*) has also been reported in ferrets and can be treated with

Sarcoptic mange: contagious skin condition caused by mites that burrow into the skin, often found on the head.

Griseofulvin 25 mg/kg for four to six weeks.

Excessive scratching may not be a sign of parasites, but instead an indication of dry skin, especially if your ferret is living in an area heated by a radiator, which makes the air very dry. A humidifier to moisten the air is one good solution to this problem, but a small amount of butter, oil, or mayonnaise may also help to alleviate this condition.

COCCIDIOSIS

Ferrets are susceptible to a number of internal parasites, including coccidia, protozoan parasites that live in the intestinal mucosa. These parasites generally do not cause any symptoms at all in healthy older animals, but they can be a serious problem in young animals or older animals that are sick or otherwise debilitated.

Animals affected by coccidia have severe diarrhea which is sometimes bloody and does not respond to antidiarrheals. Young ferrets with coccidiosis have a distinctive appearance. They are thin, with short whiskers that have been broken off close to the base, and have a very thin, dry, sparse coat. When the condition has existed for a long period of time, the anus may become red and swollen, sometimes protruding or even prolapsed.

Left untreated in symptomatic animals, coccidiosis is often fatal, and the terminal stages of this disease can be quite painful. I have heard untreated kits literally scream in pain before they finally died. (Unfortunately the diagnosis of coccidiosis was not made until an autopsy was performed.)

Coccidiosis is easily treated with antibiotics, and if treatment is begun soon enough it is almost always effective. The drug of choice is sulfadoimethoxine (Albon). The initial dose is 55 mg/kg, and then 27.5 mg/kg given orally twice daily for ten days. Rehydration with subcutaneous fluids may also be indicated if the diarrhea has been prolonged and severe. Force-feeding is seldom necessary because affected animals usually do not lose their appetite and will continue to eat on their own.

Coccidiosis is transmitted through contaminated fecal material. When treating symptomatic animals it is advisable to treat other animals in the house as well, especially those sharing the same litter pan, to avoid reexposure and reinfection with coccidia. The litter pan should be changed entirely each day and disinfected with Clorox®, which will kill coccidia shed in the feces.

To make the diagnosis, a fecal sample is examined for the presence of oocysts. Theoretically, in an animal with coccidiosis, coccidia should be seen under the microscope. This is seldom the case, however, because the rate of false negatives in fecal examinations in the ferret is unusually high. Coccidia can be shed periodically (i.e., a shower of oocysts every three or four days), making it necessary to take samples for three or four consecutive days before finally obtaining a positive one. When possible, it is preferable to test a bloody stool sample, as the stools often become bloody when oocysts are shed.

Making the diagnosis of coccidiosis, in the absence of a fecal flotation or smear positive for coccidia, requires a high index of suspicion. However, once you have seen several young ferrets with this condition, it is often possible to diagnose clinically by symptoms and general appearance of the animal, in addition to lack of response to antidiarrheals.

In my experience, coccidiosis in ferrets is a common problem which I have seen frequently. It is so common, in fact, that on numerous occasions I've made the diagnosis long distance over the telephone.

When coccidiosis is suspected clinically in the absence of a positive fecal examination, an empirical trial of sulfadimethoxine (Albon) is warranted because it can be a life-saving treatment. Sulfadimethoxine is a relatively benign drug, and although it will not do any good if the animal does not have coccidiosis, it usually will not do any harm.

Ferrets are also susceptible to other intestinal parasites such as roundworms (ascarids), which can be treated with Menbendazole 15 mg/kg, febendazole 50 mg/kg, or Ivermectin 200 mg/kg. Tapeworms are occasionally seen in ferrets and have been safely treated with praziquantel (Droncit), using 20 mg for animals weighing less than five pounds.

DIARRHEA

Diarrhea may be caused by both viral and bacterial infections. One such bacterium is *Campylobacter fetus*, subspecies *jejuni*, which may produce bloody diarrhea, anorexia (loss of appetite), and subsequent dehydration along with rectal prolapse. Treatment, which consists of rehydration with subcutaneous fluid therapy and administration of broad-spectrum antibiotics such as erythromycin, is generally unsuccessful. This infection is usually fatal in the ferret.

It is possible for other bacterial organisms, such as *Escherichia coli* and some species of the genera *Salmonella* and *Clostridia*, to cause infectious diarrhea, but this occurs only rarely in the ferret.

Ferrets are susceptible to acute episodes of viral enteritis, such as aleutian disease. Symptoms are listlessness, diarrhea, dehydration and loss of appetite. As in human viral enteritis, treatment is

supportive and symptoms should abate within five to seven days. The ferret may continue to carry the virus for as long as 200 days but will usually remain asymptomatic.

Not all diarrhea is the result of infestation with parasites. It may be caused by something as simple as a change in diet. Milk and milk products such as ice cream are notorious for causing diarrhea in ferrets because the animals are unable to digest the lactose these foods contain. (Goat's milk, incidentally, does not contain lactose and is therefore tolerated well by

ferrets.)

If diarrhea lasts longer than 24 hours and cannot be attributed to diet, or if your ferret has a fever, appears listless or ill, or refuses to eat, it is best to take your pet to a veterinarian for evaluation.

COLDS AND INFLUENZA

Ferrets are susceptible to the common cold and several strains of human influenza. Within about two days of exposure to the virus, the affected ferret will become lethargic, exhibiting a loss of appetite, fever, sneezing, and a runny nose. While

Subcutaneous: beneath the skin.

A full veterinary check-up is a good idea for a newly purchased ferret. If your pet has not yet been vaccinated against rabies, this inoculation certainly should be a part of the visit. It is imperative that ferrets be given only killed tissue rabies vaccine of murine origin.

"*Intestinal obstruction is a very common and life-threatening problem in ferrets because of their fondness for eating sponges, rubber toys, and other rubber products. . . .*"

recovery usually occurs within five days, you should take your ferret to a veterinarian whenever he has a fever, refuses to eat, or appears listless.

Wheezing breath sounds with a rapid respiratory rate may be an indication of pneumonia. Your veterinarian will be able to best decide whether or not your pet is seriously ill. In the event that he is, early treatment may save his life.

Not all sneezing is due to influenza or a cold. If your ferret is sneezing but appears active and alert and is eating well and has no other signs of illness, it is most likely that the sneezing is the result of an irritant such as dust. If your ferret has been running around under the bed or other furniture that isn't dusted under frequently, he will probably sneeze from getting dust up his nose!

INTESTINAL OBSTRUCTION

Intestinal obstruction is a very common and life-threatening problem in ferrets because of their fondness for eating sponges, rubber toys, and other rubber products such as sink stoppers, rubber bands, and baby bottle nipples, which subsequently become lodged in the intestine, leading to blockage and eventually, if left untreated, to death. In addition to their fondness for eating these potentially dangerous substances, their natural curiosity predisposes them to discovering the location of such items. Consequently, intenstinal obstruction is seen in ferrets with considerably more frequency than it is in other pets. It is so common that it is another diagnosis which I have made over the telephone on numerous occasions.

Symptoms are non-specific and include vomiting, loss of appetite, listlessness, and abdominal distension. The animal may have several bowel movements after the obstruction occurs, since there will probably be fecal matter in the intestine distal to the blockage, and this matter will continue to pass

The author's son with his ferret. They've both had their bath and now they're ready for bed.

through the intestine.

Diagnosis is best made with an abdominal x-ray, although sometimes it is possible to feel a mass in the abdomen. Ferrets very rarely vomit, so any time that a ferret presents with vomiting in addition to the above symptoms, intestinal obstruction should be considered high on the list of likely etiologies and an x-ray of the abdomen should be obtained.

Successful treatment of intestinal obstruction depends on the extent and duration of the blockage. Sometimes an enema is sufficient to remove the obstruction, but in most cases surgery is necessary. In any case, your ferret should be treated only by a veterinarian. Even if you suspect an obstruction you should *never* attempt to give your pet an enema yourself, because in doing so you could easily kill your ferret by rupturing his intestine, which may be fragile and inflamed at the site of the obstruction. If the obstruction is complete and has been present for a sufficiently long amount of time, even surgery may not be life-saving, so early diagnosis and treatment are important. If your pet displays these symptoms he should be evaluated by a veterinarian immediately.

Poisoning is another possibility that should not be overlooked in an

animal that runs free in the house or has otherwise had an opportunity to ingest a toxic substance.

As mentioned, ferrets rarely vomit, and persistent vomiting is almost always an indication of pathology such as an obstruction or a gastrointestinal tumor. Severe gastric ulcers have also been noted to cause vomiting in the ferret.

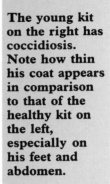

The young kit on the right has coccidiosis. Note how thin his coat appears in comparison to that of the healthy kit on the left, especially on his feet and abdomen.

Etiology: the cause or causes of a disease or condition.

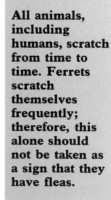

All animals, including humans, scratch from time to time. Ferrets scratch themselves frequently; therefore, this alone should not be taken as a sign that they have fleas.

MAMMARY GLAND INFECTION

Nursing ferrets sometimes develop bacterial mammary gland infections, which are relatively common. The affected gland or glands appear hot, red, firm, and swollen, and often the infection will progress to abscess formation. The responsible bacteria is most often *Staphylococcus aureus*, but can also be *Streptococcus zooepidemicas*, one of the species of *Corynebacterium* or *E. coli*. Treatment includes administration of antibiotics and a hot pack to the affected area three or four times daily to initiate drainage. Abscesses should be incised and drained. Kits should not be allowed to nurse on the infected gland. If they are not taken away from the mother entirely, the gland should be bandaged so they do not have access to it.

SPLENOMEGALY

Splenomegaly, or an enlarged spleen, is frequently seen in ferrets of all ages. It often occurs in normal, otherwise apparently healthy ferrets. It does not seem to cause these animals any problems or to shorten their life-span. At times the spleen may become so large that it will literally fill the entire abdomen. In some instances it may regress to its normal size for a period of time, then become enlarged again, and may continue indefinitely in a cycle of regression and alternate enlargement. At the present time the etiology of splenomegaly in ferrets remains a mystery and its significance is unknown. It requires no treatment, however, and a splenectomy is not indicated.

Splenomegaly may be seen in association with disease, and lymphosarcoma has been reported numerous times in the ferret. When a ferret has an enlarged spleen and other symptoms of illness, the usual attempts at diagnosis and treatment should be made. Chronic hemolytic processes as well as extramedullary hematopoiesis should be considered.

BACK PROBLEMS

Back problems are common in ferrets and may occur after trauma, but more often are present in an otherwise healthy animal with the sudden onset of paralysis of the hind limbs—either with or without accompanying urinary or fecal incontinence. This paralysis may be caused by a number of things, including hemivertebrae (a congenital malformation), intervertebral disc disease, vertebral fractures, hematomyelia (hemorrhage into the spinal cord), and myelitis (inflammation of the spinal cord).

Ferrets affected with this type of posterior paralysis who have a

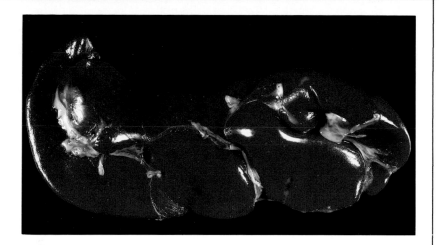

normal appearing x-ray of the spine or who have intervertebral disc problems sometimes improve considerably with steroid therapy, and 0.25 to 1 mg/kg of dexamethasone once a day can be given. Some cases do not respond to steroids, and in other cases an affected ferret will improve spontaneously without treatment. I have seen three or four male ferrets who, without treatment, have had intermittent posterior paralysis, being unaffected for long periods of time and then relapsing into paralysis only to get better and then relapse again.

HEARTWORMS

Ferrets are susceptible to heartworms, which are transmitted to them through the bite of a mosquito. Unfortunately, at this time there is no good treatment, as thiacetarsamide sodium (Carparsolate) treatment has so many bad side effects that it is more dangerous than the disease. No prophylaxis has been proved safe for ferrets, so if you live in an area where heartworms are a problem, the best way to avoid having your animals become infected is to keep them indoors and away from mosquitoes during the mosquito season.

HAIR LOSS

Ferrets sometimes have problems with alopecia, or hair loss, which can be caused by too much vitamin A or too much avidin, a protein enzyme found in raw egg albumin (egg white). Treatment in such cases is to stop feeding the offending substance to your ferret. An infrequent cause of alopecia is hypothyroidism, which can be treated with synthroid 0.02 mg/kg daily.

Other more common causes for hair loss include loss of hair before the new coat begins to grow in during a seasonal coat change and loss of hair on the ventral tail and abdomen during estrus. Both of these are normal occurrences and will resolve without treatment.

OTHER AILMENTS

Cardiomyopathy leading to congestive heart failure is not unusual in ferrets. In many instances it is the result of congenital heart defects, the incidence of which increases with inbreeding. In other cases the etiology is uncertain, but it is felt by some that dietary deficiencies may play a role in its development. The first signs may be coughing and shortness of breath, especially at night. As in other animals, this condition can often be successfully managed with a low

Prophylaxis: measures or treatments used in order to preserve the health of an animal or to control the spread of a disease.

A healthy ferret will respond to outside stimuli and will be quite playful. If your pet seems more listless than usual, a visit to the vet may be warranted.

"Ferrets should be both descented and neutered for odor control. In addition, neutering will alleviate undesirable behavior characteristics in the male and will protect the female against aplastic anemia. . . ."

Clean water and surroundings are imperative for maintaining the health of your pet or pets. Always make sure your pets are getting enough to drink.

sodium diet, lasix, and digoxin.

Ferrets are also susceptible to a wide variety of diseases and conditions seen in man and other animals, such as tuberculosis, endocrine imbalances, and various neoplasms, both malignant and benign. Diagnosis should be attempted using history, physical exam, laboratory data, pathological specimens, and x-rays, as usual. Once a diagnosis or tentative diagnosis is ascertained, treatment should be similar to that used for the cat.

STERILIZATION

Ferrets should be both descented and neutered for odor control. In addition, neutering will alleviate undesirable behavior characteristics in the male and will protect the female against aplastic anemia, which can develop as a result of prolonged estrogen exposure secondary to estrus. Ideally this surgery should be done when the ferret is six to eight weeks old. I have performed surgery on literally thousands of animals at this age and know of numerous other veterinarians and ferret breeders also doing these procedures on young ferrets, and we have had no problems from an increased incidence of anesthesia complications, changes in growth patterns, or predisposition to urolithiasis in the male. At present

Photograph of cystic prostatitis in a ferret. This is a rare disease that is not commonly found in ferrets.

there are no known contraindications to descenting or neutering a healthy kit at seven weeks of age.

Ferrets can be safely anesthetized using ketamine hydrochloride, 20 mg/kg mixed with .06 mg/kg of acepromazine. I find that the easiest way to mix this is to prepare a bottle of ketamine for use on ferrets by adding 3 mg (0.3 cc) of acepramazine to a 10 ml bottle of ketamine.

Neutering is done using the same technique as is used on the cat, and descenting is done using a technique similar to that used to descent a skunk. Needless to say, both surgery and anesthesia should be done *only* by a licensed veterinarian!

"Neutering is done using the same technique as is used on the cat, and descenting is done using a technique similar to that used to descent a skunk."

Ingestion of spongy material can cause intestinal obstruction, often resulting in death. Lightweight plastic balls are much better.

REPRODUCTION

Temperate: the climate of the regions located between the Tropic of Cancer and the arctic circle in the Northern Hemisphere or between the Tropic of Capricorn and the antarctic circle in the Southern Hemisphere.

Although reproduction is admittedly a very complex and complicated subject, taking the time to learn about the fascinating chain of events that occur during ferret reproduction can be rewarding and well worth the effort.

If you own an unspayed female, this knowledge is especially important. As the female enters the fertile phase of her reproductive cycle, she goes into a state of estrus (heat) which involves both physiological changes and willingness to accept a mate. Under natural conditions, estrus continues until sexual intercourse with a male leads to the release of oocytes (egg cell precursors), which is known as ovulation. Unfortunately, allowing a female ferret to remain in heat for a prolonged period of time is very dangerous to her health and can easily result in death. Understanding how the reproductive system functions will allow you to take the proper precautions necessary to protect the life of your female, and in addition this knowledge will increase your chances for success if you plan to breed your pets.

The ferret is especially interesting because its reproductive cycle is different from that of a dog or a cat. Like most wild animal species living in temperate climates, ferrets (even though they are not wild animals!) are seasonal breeders. When their perception of day and night is unaffected by electric lighting, ferrets reproduce only during the spring and summer of the year. This system of having the young born only in the warm weather, when food and water are usually more readily available, serves as a protective measure to increase their chances for survival and is surely nature's ingenious way of insuring the perpetuation of the species.

In the Northern Hemisphere, ferrets are sexually active for a period of about five and a half or six months—from sometime in March through the end of August. Sexual interest and preparation in females usually begins and ends later than in the males. Females generally go into heat in early April, and some may remain in that state into September. There is considerable individual variation; a small number of females go into heat as early as the end of February and go out of heat as early as July.

As one might expect, ferrets kept near the equator can breed at any time of the year, and ferrets from the United States, England, or other areas of similar latitude which are transferred to the Southern Hemisphere (South Africa or Australia) shift the onset of their breeding season by about six months.

It is only during the period of sexual activity, or estrus, that the female is receptive to the male and capable of being impregnated. At all other times she refuses sexual advances. If a male is presented to a female in estrus before he has gone into season himself, he fails to make sexual advances. In addition, he does not produce viable sperm at this time and is therefore incapable of impregnating her.

This yearly cycle of sexual activity (estrus) and inactivity (anestrus) is regulated by light/dark conditions. As the spring approaches the days increase in length and the nights become shorter. In addition, the intensity of the sunlight increases as the summer sun climbs higher in the

A group of baby ferrets relaxing in their cage. Unless you plan to breed your pets (which can be a complicated undertaking), have them altered.

It is fortunate that day length controls the readiness of the ferret to reproduce, because if another indicator such as temperature were used to signal the impending spring, unseasonably warm or cold days could easily disrupt the timing and cause the young to be born too early or too late."

Domestic ferrets were derived from the polecat, *Mustela putorius*. In the wild, the reproductive cycle of mustelids is regulated by the amount of daylight. Domestic ferrets are also affected by the light cycle, but their seasons may be influenced by electric lighting.

sky. The changes in day length and light intensity are perceived by the retinae of the ferret's eyes, and signals are transmitted to the pineal gland via the optic nerves—however, pathways different from those involved in vision are used. These messages from the environment then enter the hypothalamus (a special part of the brain), and from the hypothalamus they travel to the pituitary gland.

The pituitary gland, which is attached to the lower end of the brain, responds to these messages by secreting a hormone known as "folicle stimulating hormone," more simply known as FSH. The FSH travels through the ferret's blood stream and acts on the reproductive organs, causing them, in turn, to secrete sex hormones which enable the ferret to become sexually active.

It has been shown in various studies that neither temperature nor the gradual increase in day length affects the reproductive cycle. Instead, it is in the intensity, wavelength, and the duration of the light itself that affects the cycle, as well as the duration of the dark period.

It is fortunate that day length controls the readiness of the ferret to reproduce, because if another indicator such as temperature were used to signal the impending spring, unseasonably warm or cold days

A quintet of one-day-old ferret babies. Two to five days prior to the birth of the kits, the female may shed her winter coat; she may then use the hair in building her nest.

"Females that mate but do not conceive enter a state of pseudopregnancy in which there are hormonal changes similar to those of true pregnancy."

could easily disrupt the timing and cause the young to be born too early or too late.

There is also a regular seasonal hair, or fur, cycle in ferrets living in natural outdoor environments where light/dark conditions are unaffected by artificial lighting. This cycle is closely related to the sexual activity rhythm. The beginning of estrus and regression from it (anestrus) are correlated with the spring and autumn coat changes respectively.

In female ferrets the annual spring loss of the heavy winter coat occurs five or six weeks after the beginning of estrus. In pregnant animals, it usually precedes parturition (birth of the kits) by two to five days, and this shed hair is occasionally used in nest building. Females that mate but do not conceive enter a state of pseudopregnancy in which there are hormonal changes similar to those of true pregnancy. Hair shedding in these females often coincides with termination of an early spring pseudopregnancy.

Sometimes the dense winter coat is lost before the thinner new summer coat begins to grow in to replace it. In this case the areas where the guard hairs are normally shorter than on the rest of the body (such as the feet, lower legs and face) become almost—if not entirely—bare. Many ferret owners have called me the first time their ferret quite suddenly developed this bald appearance, concerned that there was something seriously wrong. This temporary balding does not occur in every ferret, or even the same ferret with every coat change, but when it does happen it is a part of the normal coat change and is no cause for alarm. Patience on your part is the only treatment required, since a new coat eventually grows into these areas.

Loss of the summer coat, accompanied by growth of the winter fur, begins within a week or two after the first signs of shrinking of the vulva, which marks the coming of anestrus. The time course is similar in males, in which fur coat changes accompany regression of the testes. Sometimes the new coat is almost fully grown before the old hairs of the summer coat become loose and start to shed.

The results of experiments have shown that these coat changes are affected to a considerable extent by dark/light cycles which in turn affect the activity of the pituitary gland.

A litter of week-old ferrets. Note how the coat is beginning to grow.

"'Warmth can contribute to shedding of part of the winter coat in advance of summer coat development—and thus explain why some pet ferrets living indoors or in other warm places may go through a bald period."

Although variations in temperature are much less important, they may constitute modifying factors. Warmth can contribute to shedding of part of the winter coat in advance of summer coat development—and thus explain why some pet ferrets living indoors or in other warm places may go through a bald period.

The coats of ferrets exposed to cold weather outdoors often become thicker and fuller than the coats of animals living in warmer winter environments. Spayed females and castrated males, however, do not have winter coats quite as thick as those of their intact counterparts, because they have much lower levels of the sex hormones needed to stimulate full winter coat growth. Regardless of the temperature, all ferrets, both altered and unaltered, have thicker coats during the winter period of sexual inactivity.

Ferrets also display seasonal changes in body weight which are

Three-week-old ferrets. Some details of coat coloration are starting to become noticeable.

closely associated with their sexual and coat change cycles. They begin to lose weight in the spring and can be 30 to 40 percent lighter by the end of the reproductive season.

Appetite and food intake increase markedly in the fall, and the lost weight is regained. Most of this weight is put on as a layer of subcutaneous fat, which, along with a thick winter coat, serves to help insulate the ferret against cold weather.

It should be stressed that the timing of sexual activity, coat and body weight cycles as outlined above holds true only for ferrets living outdoors under natural sunlight. This timing is often disrupted in pet ferrets living indoors and exposed to electric light after sundown. Artificially long days can cause the ferret's body to lose track of the seasons and to confuse summer with winter. As a consequence of this disruption of the normal light/dark cycles, both the male and the female can go into season at any time of the year with the usual accompanying weight loss. Most pets, however, still tend to be in heat in the spring, summer, or early fall.

Coat changes are also affected by electric lighting and coincide with the reproductive cycles, so that while they usually occur in the spring and fall, they can and do occur at any time of the year.

THE FEMALE

In the mature female hormonally induced changes leading to the onset of estrus begin when the light/dark signals occurring during early springtime are transmitted from the eyes to the hypothalamic area of the brain. The hypothalamus releases a hormone that stimulates the pituitary gland. The pituitary, in turn, secretes two hormones into the bloodstream, follicle stimulating

hormone (FSH) and luteinizing hormone (LH).

When the first of these hormones, FSH, reaches the ovary, it causes the eggs, or ova, which are produced in follicles within the ovaries, to ripen in preparation for release into the uterus. FSH, along with small amounts of LH, stimulates the ovaries to produce and release the sex hormone estrogen.

Estrogen brings about changes in both the internal and external reproductive organs. It promotes enlargement of the uterus and increases the thickness of the mucosal lining. There is considerable proliferation of uterine blood vessels and consequently a marked increase in the blood supply to that area. In addition, tiny glands that secrete mucus develop.

Externally, estrogen stimulation brings about a swelling of the vulva, which continues until the vulva is about 50 times its unstimulated size. A serous fluid is secreted, often in sufficient quantity to wet the entire underside of the hind legs, lower abdomen, and anal/tail area. (It is

The mask on the face of this 32 day-old is now becoming noticeable.

"Most pets . . . still tend to be in heat in the spring, summer, or early fall."

important to note that this thin, serous fluid is different from the thick, yellowish, foul smelling discharge that is indicative of infection.) There is an increase in body odor, even if the ferret has been descented. The undescented ferret in estrus, however, exudes a stronger smell than the descented one.

Some females in estrus will show a symmetrical loss of hair on the underside of the tail and/or abdomen. (Similar fur loss can occur in males during the normal breeding season.) The cause is unknown but is probably hormonally related and is no reason for concern, as it will grow back at the end of the breeding season or when the female goes out of heat.

The estrogen secreted by the ovaries invokes behavioral as well as physical changes in the female and causes her to be receptive to the advances of a male ferret. Most females in estrus also become a little more active than usual, but the fact

"If mating does not take place, the female remains in estrus throughout the entire breeding season, which extends from the latter part of March through July or August."

A youngster holding a baby ferret. Young children must be taught the proper way to hold any pet, and this is especially imperative when the pet is very young.

that they are in heat could easily go unnoticed by most ferret owners if it weren't for the obvious large, turgid vulva. (This will probably be appreciated by anyone who has survived one or more heat periods of a Siamese cat—or any other talkative cat, for that matter!)

If the female is bred, the stimulation provided by copulation, which includes stimulation of the neck area, increases the estrogen secretion, and this in turn causes the pituitary gland to secrete hormones in different amounts. Specifically, FSH secretion is greatly reduced and an LH "surge" occurs, during which a large amount of LH is suddenly released into the blood stream.

LH acts on the follicles of the ovaries to cause ovulation, which is the release of the oocytes. These shed oocytes move down the fallopian tubes to the fertilization site. Sperm deposited by the male travel through the vagina and uterus and some reach the same fertilization site. After a sperm cell meets and enters the oocyte, the oocyte completes its development into an ovum (egg cell) and genetic material from the male and the female intermingle. Soon after the fertilized eggs, or zygotes, form, they begin cell division. These dividing cells, the conceptus, make their way down to the uterus and implant in the uterine lining. Subsequently the implanted embryos develop rapidly into fetuses which are ready for birth six weeks after ovulation (42 days plus or minus two days).

A few days after ovulation has been induced by mating, hormonal changes cause the vulva to decrease in size.

If mating does not take place, the female remains in estrus throughout the entire breeding season, which extends from the latter part of March through July or August. Her ovaries continue to secrete estrogen

throughout this entire time, and consequently the vulva remains in its swollen condition.

This prolonged exposure to high levels of estrogen can severely damage the ferret's bone marrow cells, evoking a condition known as aplastic anemia. The bone marrow then fails to produce sufficient numbers of red blood cells (which carry oxygen to all of the tissues of the body), white blood cells (which help protect the body from infection), and platelets (necessary for normal blood clotting).

Unfortunately, aplastic anemia associated with prolonged estrus in the female ferret is invariably fatal. Out of thousands of ferrets developing this condition only two have been reported to survive.

In a female ferret in heat, the presenting signs of aplastic anemia are most often depression, lethargy, and anorexia (decreased appetite). In addition, the gums and paw pads appear pale or almost white instead of the usual healthy pink color.

Other findings can include dehydration as well as internal bleeding, which may be manifested as petechial hemorrhages (tiny hemorrhagic spots ranging in size from pin point to the size of a pin head). These are caused by extravisation, or leaking, of blood from the capillaries into the skin and mucous membranes. Ecchymosis can also occur. It differs from petechia only in that areas of extravisated blood are larger in size.

Internal bleeding is another

Ferrets generally shed twice a year, and the difference between winter coat and summer coat is more apparent in ferrets that have not been altered.

"Unfortunately, aplastic anemia associated with prolonged estrus in the female ferret is invariably fatal."

Young ferret being weighed. If you plan to breed ferrets, you must be prepared to hand feed by young if the mother becomes incapacitated for any reason.

"By the time the ferret stops eating and shows signs of listlessness, depression, and apathy, aplastic anemia has already developed."

possible consequence of aplastic anemia. Melena (passage of dark colored, tarry appearing stools), indicates that there is bleeding somewhere within the digestive tract. The stools appear dark because of the presence of blood which has been altered by the small intestine.

This internal bleeding is caused by a clotting disorder, which in turn is due to the decreased number of platelets circulating in the blood.

In addition to causing bleeding disorders, aplastic anemia disrupts the animal's immune system and thereby increases the susceptibility to bacterial infections. The infections are able to take hold more easily because the white blood cells are not present in sufficient numbers to provide their usual protection.

The enlarged vulva of the female ferret in heat, which no doubt makes the mating process easier for the

male and thus increases the chances for the female to conceive, also predisposes her to infection. The enlarged opening offers an excellent avenue for the introduction of microorganisms, and the built up mucosal lining of the uterus provides nutrients for growth of bacteria and other pathogenic organisms.

The ferret allowed to remain too long in heat is at an increased risk for the development of endometritis, or a pyometra (serious uterine infections), as a result of the effects of aplastic anemia on the immune system and the easy access to infection provided by the enlarged vulva.

Unfortunately, these infections are invariably fatal in the ferret. By the time the ferret stops eating and shows signs of listlessness, depression, and apathy, aplastic anemia has already developed. The animal cannot survive the severe anemia and is in no condition to fight off the infection.

In addition to uterine infections, the pancytopenia (reduced numbers of red cells, white cells and platelets in the blood) caused by aplastic anemia also predisposes to other types of infection, and suppurative bronchopneumonia associated with the bacteria of Klebsiella has been reported.

If infection is superimposed on anemia, your ferret may develop a fever in addition to the other symptoms. If the fever is very high, the nose will feel hot and dry to the touch. This temperature increase is eventually followed by a rapid and drastic decrease in temperature which closely precedes death.

When the uterus is infected, there is usually a thick, foul smelling, yellowish discharge from the vulva, and many times a veterinarian can feel the swollen, enlarged, pus-filled uterus within the abdomen.

Once any of these symptoms become obvious in a female ferret in estrus, the animal should be taken to a veterinarian immediately, as it is a true emergency. If you see an abnormal discharge or notice that your ferret is lethargic, and get medical attention before she stops eating, the chances for survival are somewhat better. Ideally, she should have surgery immediately and be spayed. If this is done soon enough after the development of symptoms, it may save her life. Unfortunately, by the time a ferret in heat begins to show definite signs of infections, she is also pancytopenic as a result of aplastic anemia, and is indeed very sick. Even when taken to a veterinarian post haste, her condition is usually so poor that she is unable to survive the trauma of surgery.

Most veterinarians presented with such a sick ferret will try to improve her condition medically so that she is stable enough to permit an attempt at surgical cure. Unfortunately I have not yet heard of a single ferret severely ill with a uterine infection who improved enough to survive surgery. Even such drastic measures as blood transfusions were unsuccessful in changing the invariably fatal course of this illness.

It is difficult to say just how likely it is that a female left in heat will develop aplastic anemia, with or without concurrent infection of one kind or another. Studies determining the exact numbers have not been performed, but it has been estimated that 30 to 50 percent of unspayed, unbred female ferrets die during their first estrus. There is no way to predict the fate of your pet. If you allow her to remain in heat for prolonged periods of time, you can be certain that the odds are not in her favor. Even if she is lucky enough to survive the first few breeding seasons, it is virtually guaranteed that she will not die of old age. If you care about your pet

An albino ferret. In the wild, albino animals are uncommon, as they attract the attention of predators.

"Unfortunately I have not yet heard of a single ferret severly ill with uterine infection who improved enough to survive surgery. Even such drastic measures as blood transfusions were unsuccessful in changing the invariably fatal course of this illness."

and want her to live out her full life span of eight to 12 years, you definitely won't want to play Russian roulette with her life by allowing her to stay in heat.

Complications resulting from prolonged estrus were once the leading cause of death in unaltered female pet ferrets. In years past, I regularly received countless letters and phone calls from brokenhearted ferret owners who sadly reported the recent loss of their beloved pet because they hadn't learned about the danger of letting their female remain in heat until after it was too late to save her life.

Fortunately, I rarely get these kinds of calls or letters any more. The wide distribution of my first book, the rapidly increasing popularity of ferrets as pets, and the fact that more and more veterinarians have become familiar with the animals and their physiology no doubt account for the decline in incidence of this fatal problem.

If you don't want to let your ferret have kits, the ideal way to protect her health is to have her spayed so that she won't ever go into heat. This is such a good solution that both of the largest breeders of pet ferrets in the United States, and even some of the smaller breeders, are now selling only spayed females.

Another advantage to spaying is that neutered females have somewhat less odor than unaltered females, even in the winter when the unaltered females are not in heat. There is no noticeable change in the behavior or personality of a spayed female. The only differences you will find are that the altered female may not grow quite as thick a winter coat and won't show as much seasonal color change. In many ferrets this attenuation of color is most noticeable in the failure to develop a prominent mask in the winter.

Not spaying your ferret makes sense only if you want her to have kits. You can safely bring your female out of heat and protect her health during cycles in which she is not bred by having her injected with ovulation-inducing hormones.

An injection of 100 USP units of chorionic gonadatropin, which acts like LH to promote ovulation and terminate estrus, can be used for this purpose. This injection should be given after the vulva reaches full size, usually about two weeks after your first notice that it is beginning to swell. If this hormone has induced ovulation, the vulva should begin to decrease in size within about one week, and then continue to get smaller. If after a week the vulva shows no sign of shrinking, a second dose of 100 USP units should be given. If there is still no sign of regression in the size of the vulva the following week, a third dose of 200 USP units can be tried.

Alternatively, progesterone (Depoprovera), a different hormone which has the advantage of being more readily available and less expensive, can be used for this purpose. The dosage is still controversial; however, 10 mg has been used successfully, which can be increased to 15 mg should a second or third dose be required.

If both chorionic gonadatropin and progesterone are unavailable, Ovaban, a synthetic progestin used as a cat birth control pill, can be given instead. The initial dose is 15 mg, and 30 mg if a second or third dose is required. (Interestingly enough, this same method of using hormones to terminate estrus also works well on the family cat in heat, although the dosage required is larger! As in ferrets, these hormones should be given to your cat only under the supervision of a licensed veterinarian.)

Occasionally, a ferret shows no

sign of going out of heat after two or three doses of hormone. In these instances I strongly recommend that you stop playing around with hormones and find a male ferret to do the job of terminating your pet's estrus condition! This is a fool-proof method as long as the male you are using is mature and sexually active. Although it may result in pregnancy, it is preferable to the continued risk of infection and death.

Induction of ovulation with hormones or by a sterile mating (copulation with a male not producing viable sperm) will cause your ferret to have a pseudopregnancy, or pseudocyesis. During this false pregnancy, the uterus and mammary glands undergo the same changes as they do during a true pregnancy. Although in both conditions the vulva decreases to approximately one-fourth of the estrus size, it does not regress completely. Pseudocyesis, or pseudopregnancy, lasts the same length of time as a true pregnancy, about six weeks. Within a few weeks

after the end of a pseudopregnancy, your ferret will probably go into heat again unless it is her second or third heat of the season and/or very late in the breeding season. If your ferret does not go into heat a second time seven or eight weeks after ovulation, the vulva will regress to its normal anestrus size.

THE MALE

The male ferret, like the female, is not capable of reproducing year round. During the winter months his testes are inactive. The hormone secreting cells make very little testosterone (the male sex hormone), and the Sertoli cells, which are needed to promote maturation of spermatozoa, are small.

Changes in natural lighting beginning in the spring initiate a period of heightened sexual activity, during which mature sperm are produced. First, FSH is released from the pituitary gland. It travels through the bloodstream to the testes, where it stimulates the growth of the Sertoli cells. These cells then become capable of protecting, nourishing, and encouraging the growth of sperm cells. At the same time LH is also released from the pituitary gland. This hormone causes the testes to begin producing and secreting testosterone into the blood stream. The level of testosterone in the body builds up gradually, and until a certain critical level is reached, the male shows no sexual interest or activity. When testosterone levels rise sufficiently, the male begins to display sexual behavior such as mounting of the female.

While moderate amounts of testosterone may stimulate mating behavior, they must reach an even higher critical level in order to promote formation of mature sperm.

Whether you plan to own one ferret or to operate a ferret breeding establishment, you must be able to handle your ferrets comfortably and properly.

"The male ferret, like the female, is not capable of reproducing year round."

"Two unaltered males who were not kept together while they were coming into season will fight and may seriously injure one another when put together."

Consequently it is possible for the male to mate before his hormone levels are high enough to cause the production of sperm. At this stage, sterile mating can occur. This means that copulation can stimulate ovulation in the female, but she will not conceive and become pregnant.

Although it is easy to tell if a female has come into season by observing the condition of her vulva, it is considerably more difficult to determine whether or not a male has achieved fertility. The changes which occur in the male come about more slowly and they are more subtle than those which occur in the female.

During the winter period of sexual inactivity, the testes are small, soft, and in a forward position in the groin. As the male begins to come into season, the testes move back into the scrotum, just in front of the anus. At the same time they begin to enlarge and become turgid. The hair thins over the testes until, at the time of greatest testis size, the scrotum is almost bare and the animal is ready for fertile matings.

When the male ferret begins to go out of season, testosterone levels gradually fall. Sperm production ceases before sexual interest wanes, and sterile mating is again possible.

If you are not going to use your male for breeding, it is best to have him castrated. There are several reasons for this, the most compelling of which is odor. Male ferrets that have not been castrated have a very strong odor, even if they have been descented. Most people find the smell so unpleasant that they cannot tolerate having an unaltered male indoors as a house pet. (Since I didn't have a backyard in New York City, I opted to keep my studs in a large cage outside the kitchen window of my apartment!)

In addition to the unpleasant odor, non-castrated males have several undesirable habits such as urinating in little "spots" all over the house, which they do to claim territories. Many tend to be hyperactive and overexcitable. Some are rough when interacting with people, and they have been known to bite. A sexually active male will mount and bite the neck of a female even when she is not in heat, and will mount castrated males in the same manner. Two unaltered males who were not kept together while they were coming into season will fight and may seriously injure one another when put together.

Because there are so many problems associated with having unaltered male ferrets, they do not make very good house pets, and you are better off keeping a castrated male and seeking stud service for your female whenever you wish to breed her.

The author, her son, and two ferrets. Before planning to breed your ferrets, learn as much as you can about their reproductive systems and gain some experience in keeping them as pets. It will also be helpful to find a knowledgeable ferret breeder to whom you can turn for advice.

BREEDING

*"The chances of
a successful
mating resulting
in pregnancy are
best between
April and July
or August."*

**Profile of an
albino ferret.
Breeding ferrets
for color and
type is a
fascinating
undertaking,
but it is not
recommended
for novices.**

BREEDING

Most pet ferrets who live indoors are
subjected, along with the rest of the
family, to electric lighting after
sundown. This has the effect of
increasing the length of their day.
Since day length controls the cycle of
sexual activity and inactivity in
ferrets, artificially long days can
cause both the male and the female
to come into season at any time of
the year. In addition, there are
individual differences in the
response of each ferret to light, and
several animals living under the
same lighting conditions may go into
season weeks or even months apart.
For this reason, male and female
sexual activity cycles frequently do
not coincide during either the winter
or early and late in the natural
breeding season. The chances of a
successful mating resulting in
pregnancy are best between April
and July or August. This is the
natural breeding season and the time
when most pets tend to be in heat at
the same time.

Ferrets in an environment of
natural sunlight become sexually
mature the first spring following
their birth, or when they are eight to
ten months old. Ferrets born in the
winter or ferrets kept under artificial
lighting, however, can undergo
accelerated maturation and become
capable of reproducing at as early as
four months of age.

Even though females can go into
heat as many as three or four times a
year (especially those kept under
electric lights), it is probably best to
breed them only once a year. The
physical stress of having two or three

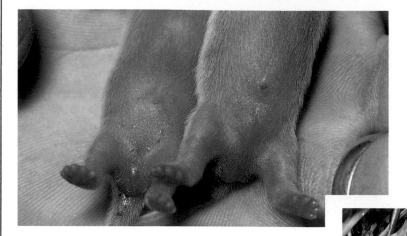

Left: A closeup of two-day-old ferrets, a male and a female.

Right: A cluster of two-day-old ferrets in the nest.

Above: A pair of two-day-old ferrets.

Right: Ferret kits, like human babies, grow very quickly. Note the difference in the sizes of these two kits.

Left: A pair of nine-day-old ferrets. Note how the colors are already easy to distinguish.

litters a year may significantly shorten their life span.

Optimally, females should be bred when the vulva has reached its maximum size. This usually occurs about two weeks after the swelling is first noticeable.

The only sure way of knowing if a sexually active male is fully in season and producing viable sperm in sufficient numbers to impregnate a female is to look at his ejaculate under a microscope. The increased size and rearward position of the testes does, however, give some indication.

Courtship of a female in full estrus by a potent male is very rough and at times even violent. Although it may look to you as if the female is in danger of being killed, this behavior is normal for ferrets.

Using his teeth, the male grasps the female by the nape of the neck, not infrequently breaking the skin and causing her to bleed. The female becomes almost passive as the male throws her back and forth and drags her about on the ground.

In time she becomes more and more submissive. When she is almost completely limp, the male, still gripping her by the back of the neck, throws her on her side and holds her in place with his front and hind legs while he attempts entry. This can take anywhere from several minutes to half an hour.

After successful entry and copulation, the animals may remain locked in position for as long as three hours. On separation the male may either be left with the female or removed. If they are left together, further matings are likely to occur.

One successful copulation induces ovulation in the female, and if the male was fertile, pregnancy may result. If the male is not fully in season (not producing viable sperm), a sterile mating can occur. The female will nevertheless ovulate, but a pseudopregnancy (false pregnancy) will follow.

Both pregnancy and pseudopregnancy evoke similar hormonal changes in the female. These include enlargement of the uterus and mammary glands. It is very difficult to tell the difference between these two conditions until about three weeks after the mating, when an experienced handler will be able to feel the fetuses growing within the uterus.

THE PREGNANT FEMALE

After you breed your female, you should care for her as if she were pregnant, even though it may be three or four weeks before you know for certain whether the mating was successful.

Your ferret will have an increased appetite at this time, and she should be allowed to eat as much as she wishes. Take special care to ensure that she is getting a balanced diet. She will also probably want to sleep a lot more; this is normal.

Although the vulva decreases in size significantly after she becomes pregnant, it remains somewhat swollen, and you may see a thick mucous discharge from the vagina. As long as this discharge is not yellow or foul smelling, it is normal and no cause for concern. If it is yellow or brownish and/or foul smelling, however, it may be an indication of infection, and she should be taken to a veterinarian as soon as possible.

Four or five weeks after ovulation is induced, either by breeding or hormones, and regardless of whether or not she is pregnant, the female begins to shed her winter coat. She may do this slowly over a long period of time, or it may come out all at once by the handful. Some ferrets use the shed hair in building a nest for their kits. Sometimes new

"After you breed your female, you should care for her as if she were pregnant, even though it may be three or four weeks before you know for certain whether the mating was successful."

summer coat growth can be seen close to the skin before the winter fur has been shed. Another possibility is that the new coat may not begin to grow out until several weeks after shedding of the old, leaving the animal with a thin, scraggly appearance.

The pregnant female, for the most part, can continue with life as usual until a few days before her kits are

good, because you need to be able to check frequently on both mother and kits to be sure that all is well. In addition, your pet may choose somewhere totally unreasonable to keep her kits, such as in one of your dresser drawers, inside the stuffing of the sofa, or in the dirty laundry hamper.

You should introduce your pregnant female to the idea of living

due. (Although Melinda and McGuinn didn't work, they did go to school right up until the day their babies were born!)

If your pet has free run of the house, it is a good idea to confine her to a cage or a small area during the last two weeks of her pregnancy and until the kits are weaned, otherwise she may (like many cats) hide her kits or move them about from place to place. This is not

in a cage or small area several weeks before her kits are due, because if you wait until they are born to confine her, she may become so upset at losing her freedom that she will ignore her babies entirely and concentrate on escaping. If she is confined for gradually longer periods of time each day, starting several weeks before she gives birth, by the time the kits finally arrive she will have become accustomed to the

A 16-day-old ferret.

restriction and can turn her full attention to her new family.

Her cage or small area should contain a bed or "nest box." An ordinary cardboard box is fine if you cut down one side a little so she won't overturn it when climbing in and out. A clean towel can be used for bedding. It should be large enough for your pet to cover herself and her kits, but not so large that the kits get lost in it.

As the due date for the birth of the kits draws near, both the pregnant and the pseudopregnant female look and act pregnant. Some females become overly affectionate, and they may lick your hands and/or face incessantly—almost as if they are practicing their mothering skills on you! During the sixth and last week of a true pregnancy, however, if you rest your fingers lightly on the side of your pet's abdomen and exercise great patience, you should be able to feel the unborn kits moving inside of their mother, and you will know for certain that your ferret is pregnant.

It is usually all right to leave the stud with your female while she is pregnant, as long as he does not bother her with sexual advances. I recommend separating them a few days before the kits are due, however, because while some studs have been known to exhibit friendly behavior toward their offspring, licking them and appearing to help take care of them, others have been known to kill them.

Care should also be taken when letting other adult ferrets around the kits until you can ascertain how they are going to respond to them. McGuinn killed one of Melinda's babies when I put it in the cage with her. Although she had been spayed for about a year at the time, it did not occur to me that she might have lost her mothering instinct. I was

"As the due date for the birth of the kits draws near, both the pregnant and the pseudopregnant female look and act pregnant."

Ferret kits, 23 days old, sleeping inside their straw nest. Young ferrets do little more than sleep and eat during the first few weeks of life.

"Some ferret 'mothers' without kits choose to adopt another adult animal, and have been known to be a complete nuisance to other ferrets living in the same household. . . ."

quite surprised at her vicious behavior, since she had had three litters of her own prior to being spayed and had been a very good mother.

FALSE PREGNANCY

If your female ferret goes through a pseudopregnancy (false pregnancy), she will most likely begin to behave like a mother at about the time she would have had her kits—at the end of what would have been the six-week gestation period. Since she has no kits of her own to care for, she will probably adopt.

Ferrets, like dogs and other animals who have had a false pregnancy, sometimes adopt inanimate objects and treat them as if they were babies.

Following one of her false pregnancies, Sally dragged a towel out of the cat bed and used it to build herself a nice little nest in the corner of my bedroom closet. She then gathered up all the ferret toys in the house and put them in her nest. She tried to keep all of the other ferrets out of the closet, but on occasion one of them would get in and steal one of her "kits," and she would dutifully run after the offending ferret, scolding it all the while with a worried, soft clucking sound, retrieve the toy "baby," and quickly return it to the safety of her nest. She kept watch over all her "kits" in this manner for almost a week before she finally lost interest and gave up returning them to the closet when they were stolen.

Some ferret "mothers" without kits choose to adopt another adult animal, and have been known to be a complete nuisance to other ferrets living in the same household— licking them, washing their ears, and trying to drag them off by the scruff of the neck.

If there are no other ferrets in the house, your ferret may even choose you to be her baby—licking you incessantly, following you around, and otherwise just generally making a pest of herself. This can be a very trying period for everyone involved.

Shortly after a false pregnancy, one ferret I know, Possum, became a terrible bother to her owner, David. She repeatedly picked up his thumb very gently between her teeth and tried to carry it off and put it under the sofa, clucking softly all the while. We never did figure out if she was planning to use his thumb for a baby (it was about the right size and shape!) or if she was just using it to move David to her nest so she could use him for the baby. Either way she was quite unhappy when she couldn't get his thumb to stay under the sofa!

Melinda adopted me once when it became necessary for me to take her litter of six kits away from her for a few days while I treated her for a mammary gland infection. She made a real pest out of herself by continually climbing up on me and licking me on the neck, so I was more than a little happy when her infection had cleared up enough for her to nurse her kits again. Naturally, I assumed that since she had her babies again she would leave me alone and go back to taking care of them instead. I was a bit surprised when I woke up the first night after I returned them to her to find her licking my neck. I was even more surprised when I looked down and saw her six babies curled up on my pillow right underneath my chin. She had adopted me and evidently she wanted to keep me. Not only that, but she obviously wanted to have her entire family together. Since I was too big for her to move into the nest with her babies, the only thing she could do was to move her babies into the bed with me! I

You may prefer to give your female ferret a basket lined with cloth to use as a nest for raising her young, or you may give her clean towels and other materials and let her make her own.

put her and her babies back in their nest several times that night, only to wake and find that she once again moved them all back into bed with me. She was so insistent that we all sleep together that I finally had to shut her out of the bedroom.

The ideal solution for a ferret mother having no kits of her own is to adopt someone else's. When Melinda had a false pregnancy, it was no surprise to me that she immediately adopted McGuinn's litter of eight babies.

Although she had no milk and couldn't nurse them, she happily helped McGuinn take care of them. Everything went well for the first several weeks; both mothers stayed in the nest box with the kits almost all of the time. As the kits got bigger and more demanding, though, McGuinn, who had to take all the responsibility for nursing them, started wanting to get away for an occasional nap outside the nest box. Melinda, however, included McGuinn among her adopted brood and refused to let McGuinn leave the nest box. Every time poor McGuinn got out, Melinda grabbed her by the scruff of the neck and hauled her right back in!

Melinda insisted that McGuinn stay with the rest of her litter at all times and persisted in this behavior so relentlessly that she finally had to be locked out of the cage. In addition, the method of closing the cage had to be changed from leather ties to metal snaps, because she soon learned to untie the leather knots with her teeth while hanging from her paws on the side of the cage. Then she would push the door open with her nose and go back in! This maneuver usually took her a very long time, but she always persisted until she succeeded because she wanted so very much to get back to her "babies."

Actually, ferrets don't even have to be "kitless" to want to adopt kits. Melinda had a litter of her own when Artful Dodger, who belonged to my friend Iris, had a litter of 13 kits. Since Arty couldn't very well nurse 13 kits, we decided to see if we could interest Melinda in taking care of a few of them for her.

We needed a way to tell Melinda's kits from Arty's kits, so we decided to mark Arty's kits with a spot of non-toxic dye. Before we could even get the bottle of dye open, however, Melinda came running into the room and tried to take the kit I was holding. She was so eager to add those kits to her litter that Iris had to hold her while I marked them with dye. When I finished and Iris turned her loose, she gently took each kit and quickly carried it off to her nest box, scolding us with a soft clucking sound—as if we had stolen them from her and she was finally getting them back!

Melinda was an exceptionally good

"The ideal solution for a ferret mother having no kits of her own is to adopt someone else's."

mother and seemed to be especially crazy about babies, but I have heard of numerous other "baby crazy" ferrets. Several ferret mothers I know, who live in the same household and have had litters at the same time, regularly took turns stealing each other's kits—as if eight weren't enough.

BIRTH AND CARE OF THE KITS

Female ferrets generally suffer no complications while giving birth. Nature has equipped them with the instinct to undergo this experience alone, without the aid of concerned human midwives. If your ferret has a calm disposition and a close, trusting attachment to you, she probably won't discourage your presence. Keep in mind, however, that even the friendliest, most gentle ferret mother does not like to have her babies handled. Keep all curious humans (especially children) at a safe distance from the babies. Unless it is absolutely necessary, do not handle the babies. If for some reason you must pick one up, the mother ferret, contrary to folklore, will not kill because it has acquired a human scent. The babies themselves are quite hardy and can be handled without harm soon after birth.

THE FIRST LITTER

Some first-time ferret mothers don't seem to know what is happening to them. They may even get confused and run into the litter pan to give birth to the first kit. When this happens, you can help by picking her up and gently placing her back in the nest box. Some advance preparation of the birth area on your part will also help to make things easier for the inexperienced mother. Make sure that she has a comfortable nest box with clean

A demonstration of the proper way to hold a young ferret for feeding. Remember that hand-feeding is a less desirable option than having another ferret mother adopt the orphans.

"Some ferrets will attack any hand or inquisitive face that approaches the newborns."

bedding. The area should be warm, quiet, and free from other pets or people. Again, you should bear in mind that any handling of the kits could be hazardous to the handler. It depends solely on the nature of the mother ferret. Some mothers like Melinda will gently take the kit away from you if you attempt to pick it up. Some ferrets will attack any hand or inquisitive face that approaches the newborns. A friend of mine can attest to this, having been nipped on the nose for merely taking a peek at McGuinn's newborn kits.

THE BIRTH

At birth, the kits will be enclosed in an amniotic sac as they emerge from the birth canal. In many cases, this thin, membranous, fluid-filled bag will break and be pushed aside during delivery. If the bag does not break at birth, it is the mother's natural instinct to lick it away from the face of the kit to allow breathing. On occasion, ferret mothers, usually with their first litter, may neglect this vital chore. If you should observe a baby still enclosed in the sac after ten or 15 seconds have gone by, you can prevent its death from suffocation. Gently stroke the kit's face and nose with the corner of a clean, damp cloth. This will clear the membrane from the face, enabling the newborn kit to breathe. Shortly thereafter he will begin to cry.

BAD MOTHERS

One problem that may occur at birth is cannibalism. For some unexplained reason, the mother may devour the entire litter one at a time. This cannibalism has nothing to do with the presence or absence of the pet owner. It poses a tough problem. To survive, the kits must be taken from the parent immediately. Once removed from the mother, the kits will not live long. Their only hope is for you to find another ferret with a newborn litter or one about to give birth. If placed in the protective care of this new mother, the displaced kits will be nursed and raised along with the other true members of her litter.

Another problem of ferret motherhood is equally strange. A mother may totally disregard her first litter and instead focus all her mothering instincts on others. I've known of instances where the ferret tried to mother other adult ferrets in the household. In another case, the ferret tried to mother the owner. The kits did not survive. This behavior occurred only during first-time motherhood. On the second litter these same ferrets became excellent, caring mothers.

The arrival time of the newborns as well as the litter size can be varied. Kits may emerge every five or ten minutes, or there may be an hour or more between the arrival of each kit. If the mother is upset, the time between births may be lengthened. Occasionally the last kit will be born as much as a day or more later than the rest of the litter. Some births may cover several hours but still be comparatively smooth. Longer births spanning an entire day or more have occurred. Prolonged delivery is usually accompanied by pain and upset in the mother.

Litter sizes average around five or six. Litters have been recorded with as few as one or as many as 14. The largest litter I've heard of numbered 22, an incredibly rare event.

Like many other mammals, the kits are born with eyes closed. At birth, their skin is smooth, pink, and seemingly devoid of hair. Their thin layer of fine white fuzz will appear as the baby dries off.

Normally the kits will start nursing within several hours of birth. If you do not notice any

nursing activity after several hours, it is possible that the mother has not produced any milk. The only chance for survival of the kits, in this case, will be to quickly place them with a nursing foster mother.

BRINGING UP THE KITS

For a few weeks, the mother will reside in the nest with the newborns, leaving only for quick trips to the litter box and food dish. During their first weeks you will observe many changes in the kits. Their pinkish color will gradually disappear as their fuzzy white coat grows thicker. It is still too early to observe the distinct markings of a White-foot, a Sable, or a Butterscotch, but at this time you will be able to administer the albino test. Look through the thin, sealed eyelids. Inside should be a distinct dark spot, the iris. If no spot is seen, the kit has red eyes, the markings of an Albino, also known as a Red-eyed White. With that exception, all other kits will darken as they grow. White fur will gradually give way to light gray and then to gray-brown.

After three weeks, little eyes will begin to open. The larger the litter, the sooner the kits will open their eyes—for some mysterious reason. Small litters will take about a month for eye-opening.

At three weeks, the babies are ready to start eating semi-solid food. A mushy mixture of canned cat food and a simulated mother's milk product available in pet stores should be placed in the nest several times daily. The kits will already have tiny, sharp teeth, even though their eyes may not yet be open. This will allow the mother some rest time between the constant feedings. During this six to seven weeks of nursing, the mother will eat much more than usual. All her nourishment, however, will be going to the kits. As a result, the mother may gradually lose weight and become run down. Starting the kits on semi-solid food will be a welcome relief for her. If you forget to put mush in the nest box, many times the mother will bring food in herself from her dish.

HOUSEKEEPING

When the kits begin taking the semi-solid mush, there will be a continuous messy buildup of food bits and excrement in the nest. The mother will do her best to keep the kits personally clean, but you should maintain good sanitary conditions in the nest area. The cardboard nest box should be replaced every few days. Remains of food from previous feedings should be cleaned out before the next feeding, because the old mush will spoil or sour. If it is eaten, the kits may become very sick and possibly even die.

Weaning, the gradual withdrawal of the kits from their nursing routine, should commence at about six weeks of age. You can help by first separating the largest kits from the mother. Follow this each day by separating the next largest, and so on, until the mother is free from the stresses of nursing. She will then cease production of milk and enjoy a more relaxed, comfortable life.

After the entire litter has been weaned, the mush mixture (canned cat food and simulated mother's milk) can be supplemented with bits of dry cat chow.

"Weaning, the gradual withdrawal of the kits from their nursing routine, should commence at about six weeks of age."

SAFETY

"Even with the tiny warning bells they wear on their collars to alert me to their presence, they still get a toe or tail trod upon or a kick in the nose every now and then—to which they respond vocally with what sounds a bit like cursing in Chinese!"

Because of their small size, undying curiosity, and natural tendency to burrow and crawl into and under things, ferrets are subject to numerous safety hazards both in the home and out of doors. Before you even bring your ferret home, it is important that you ferret-proof all rooms in which your pet will be allowed to run free by blocking up all holes and crevices through which he will disappear if given the chance.

DON'T TREAD ON ME

One major danger for ferrets is that they are easily stepped on. They are so small and quiet that frequently you won't see or hear them approach. If you aren't careful to look where you step, you may accidentally injure your little pet. My ferrets are continually underfoot as they follow me around the house. Even with the tiny warning bells they wear on their collars to alert me to their presence, they still get a toe or tail trod upon or a kick in the nose every now and then—to which they respond vocally with what sounds a bit like cursing in Chinese!

Because ferrets love to burrow, they will frequently crawl under a rug, the corner of a blanket, or an article of clothing left on the floor. It may turn out to be a disaster for your little critter if you walk on something he is napping under! Try to keep closets, trunks, and drawers closed, as these are also favorite places for napping and your pet could easily become imprisoned in them.

Another hazard of burrowing and crawling into holes and small spaces is that occasionally a ferret will get his head, shoulder, or leg firmly wedged in between two surfaces and be unable to free himself. I have rescued McGuinn from such situations twice, once when she had her head caught between the radiator and the wall, and another time when she had her head caught between a board in my closet and the wall. Both times she had been missing for at least 12 hours before I found her, and I'm sure that she was caught so firmly that she could not have gotten loose without my help.

Robynn and Jerry Huffman of Independence, Missouri, recently wrote to tell me about a similar, but much worse, situation involving their ferret, Smitty.

"On Sunday night about 9pm we were gathering the animals for bed and only found the two girls, Sadie and Satchel. We looked for Smitty through every drawer and under every piece of furniture. He just wasn't there. Then we remembered that earlier in the day we had the front door open while we were bringing in the groceries. We decided he must have gotten out, so we put ads in the local paper. The week that he was gone we sometimes thought we were hearing his bell, but we were so sure he'd gotten out the door we decided we must be just imagining it.

"After he had been gone for eight days we heard his bell in the laundry room, this time too loud to be just imagination. We looked all over the laundry room but still didn't find him. We took a break from our search to have lunch, and while we were eating, a friend came over to use our washing machine. She came out of the laundry room and asked, 'Do ferrets squeak? If they do I think Smitty is in the washing machine.'

"Sure enough he had gotten in the

Providing your ferret with safe toys and a safe area to play in is an important part of being a responsible pet owner.

washer and had somehow gotten pinned in. After eight days of having no food or water he was just barely alive. His eyes were dull and sunken and he couldn't walk. We took him to the emergency clinic with very little hope—he was in such bad shape we didn't see how he could possibly make it. But somehow, miraculously, he pulled through, and now he's fine except for his left front leg, which was wedged into a tight space for so long that it was permanently paralyzed."

SMOTHERING

Even though I was aware of some of the dangers ferrets encounter because of their burrowing tendencies, I was unprepared for what happened to McGuinn!

I was awakened one morning by the movement of the mattress at the foot of my bed. I got up to investigate and discovered that McGuinn had crawled in between the two mattresses in my sleeping loft and was curling up for a nap. I thought that she had chosen a very strange place to snooze, but because she and my other ferrets frequently crawled inside the pillowcase or under my pillow to sleep, I didn't think anything about it and just got up and went to the library, leaving her there.

When I came home later and called the ferrets, Melinda came out to meet me and Sally finally came out to eat about an hour later. I wondered where McGuinn was, but assumed she was already sleeping soundly somewhere and didn't start to worry until later that night when she still hadn't appeared. Feeling that she might be hung up by her collar or otherwise trapped or in trouble somewhere, I started looking for her. I searched for almost ten minutes before I remembered where I'd seen her last that morning. Sure enough I found her there, curled up between the two mattresses in my sleeping loft. She had gone to sleep and slept so soundly that she smothered to death after she had used up all the oxygen. Evidently the mattress was heavy enough to keep the fresh air from reaching her.

ACCIDENTAL INJURIES

Reclining chairs and convertible sofa beds are also potential dangers for the ferret who crawls underneath or inside them for a nap. Unfortunately, I know of several such ferrets who were crushed to death by unsuspecting owners.

Some ferrets like to crawl into or underneath the washing machine or clothes dryer. These places should be off limits to your pet, but care should be taken not to wash, dry, or otherwise injure him in case he occasionally trespasses. I recently

"Reclining chairs and convertible sofa beds are . . . potential dangers for the ferret who crawls underneath or inside them for a nap."

Ferrets were often used to catch rabbits because of their superior burrowing abilities. It is important for the pet owner to be aware of the ferret's tendencies to enter holes and disappear.

Ferrets are naturally curious and will play just about anywhere. They should be kept out of unsuitable areas, such as public drinking fountains.

heard of a ferret who met an unfortunate end when she got washed in the dishwasher. Apparently she had crawled in to investigate, and it didn't occur to her owner to check inside for a curious ferret before he turned on the machine.

I also know of a ferret who met an equally tragic fate when she crawled into a pile of dirty clothes for a nap. She was sleeping so soundly that she didn't wake up when the clothes were transferred from the floor to the machine, and was sadly discovered too late, after the clothes had been washed.

Clothes dryers can pose other hazards to ferrets, as my friend Linda Smothers found out—the hard way.

"Dick and I were staying with friends at their condo in Lake Tahoe last winter and I had all three ferrets with me.

"Our friends had a bathroom/laundry room where I let the ferrets out to play. The dryer wasn't working and had been pulled out from the wall and the large vent hose disconnected from the dryer. The hose led down under the condo and was just laying on the floor. The morning we were leaving it was snowing really hard. I went to get the ferrets back in their cage and ready to leave, but I couldn't find Wally (Melinda's son) anywhere. In the meantime Alvin kept running

into the dryer hose and back out, looking very perturbed. I hadn't realized that the disconnected hose led down under the condo, but with Alvin's peculiar behavior I asked the owner about it. He said it went somewhere under the building but he wasn't sure where.

"I went outside in the blizzard to try to figure out where the hose comes out. After pulling off all the boards and paneling from the side of the building, I could finally see into this three-foot high crawl space—

"I recently heard of a ferret who met an unfortunate end when she got washed in the dishwasher."

If you plan to take your ferrets outside, be sure you supervise them at all times.

Comedian Dick Smothers sharing a banana with Wally the ferret and Custer the parrot.

"Another danger for the pet ferret is the ignorance of neighbors. Although ferrets are certainly more popular than they were several years ago and more people are familiar with them, there are still many people who don't have any idea what a ferret is."

and there sits Wally, all covered with dirt and dryer fuzz and looking very bewildered and cold. So I crawled in and got him and apologized profusely for causing so much trouble. I've never been so panicked in my life! And then later it was just really embarrassing! And if that wasn't enough, not long afterwards Whitney got behind my dryer at home and clawed at the hose until he pulled it out of the wall. Then he climbed in the hole and dropped down four or five feet. Dick had to crawl down under the house to get him. Poor Whitney was really scared and never did anything like that again. (Dick also did a good job of plugging up the hole!)"

Several ferrets I know have been known to crawl unnoticed into the refrigerator, and although they did make enough noise to attract the attention of their owners, they also made a big mess!

NEIGHBORS

Another danger for the pet ferret is the ignorance of neighbors. Although ferrets are certainly more popular than they were several years ago and more people are familiar with them, there are still many people who don't have any idea what a ferret is. If your pet happens to slip out the door or otherwise get out of your house or apartment, he may be unlucky enough to encounter someone who thinks he is a rat or other wild animal and get beaten to death with a broomstick!

COLLARS AND IDs

To help protect your ferret against many of these dangers, it is a good idea to have your pet wear a collar with an identification tag and a small bell. He probably won't like the idea at first and will try to scrape it off, pull it off, or outrun it, but after 15 minutes or so it won't bother him any more and he'll definitely be much safer.

The bell will serve as a locator to tell you when he's underfoot so that you can avoid stepping on him. It can also help you find him if he's caught somewhere or has accidentally gotten locked up in something. In addition, it may alert you to the fact that he's on his way out the door when you might not have seen him or noticed him if he'd been silent.

In the event that he does get out of the house unnoticed, the collar and bell will indicate that whatever the animal is, it must be someone's pet, so hopefully he won't be killed by the first terrified person he saunters up to and attempts to befriend. I don't know if Melinda would have been killed had she not been wearing a collar, but it did definitely identify her as a pet when I first moved to Cincinnati, Ohio, to go to medical school. I had left the back door open while I was moving my belongings from the car into my new apartment. When I discovered that the ferret's cage was open, I quickly searched the house and made a ferret count. After ten minutes all ferrets were accounted for and back in the cage, except Melinda, who had evidently gone out the door. The backyard was large and extended for a distance of about 50 yards. The farthest section was heavily wooded and covered with thick tall grass and brush. I called and called to no avail, which really didn't surprise me, because when given the opportunity to explore something new and different, all of my ferrets become temporarily deaf and won't even consider coming when I call them. I searched the woods frantically for a while, fearing that Melinda would run into an unfriendly dog or that some equally disastrous mishap would befall her before I could find her. Finally it occurred to me that

she might not have gone into the woods, but instead might have stayed around the house or gone in the direction of the house next door. As I neared the front I heard voices coming from the porch of the house two doors down. As I got closer I could hear a woman saying "Maybe it's a mole," to which another woman replied, "Well, I don't know what it is but it's got to be somebody's pet—it's wearing a collar." I knew immediately that I'd found Melinda and was tremendously relieved that she was safe, but I must say that I was more that a little surprised to walk up on the porch and find Melinda happily digging in the woman's potted plant, throwing dirt all over the place. I still don't know why that dirt was more appealing than the dirt all over the yard!

In addition to identifying your ferret as a pet, a collar with an identification tag may help get your ferret returned to you. I know of numerous people who have gotten a call from a neighbor who found their pet and were brave enough to pick it up and get the phone number from the collar. I also get calls from people who say they've found a ferret that looks well cared for and is obviously someone's pet, but they don't know where it lives or who it belongs to, and they want to know if I know of anyone who has lost one. Unfortunately, most of these ferrets found without an ID tag never make it home again.

The collar should be reasonably thin and lightweight; a kitten collar cut down to a smaller size works well and can be purchased at any pet store. Perhaps as ferrets become even more popular, pet stores will begin to sell ferret collars! Leather, suede, or nylon are better than plastic, which frays when you cut it. While you can use a safety collar that has an elastic piece in it which allows

"In addition to identifying your ferret as a pet, a collar with an identification tag may help get your ferret returned to you."

Keeping your ferret on a leash when it is outdoors is the best way to keep it from getting into trouble.

"Care should be taken to keep all dangerous toys and sponges out of reach of ferrets—sponges kept under the sink seem to be especially popular with and easily located by most ferrets."

Since holes and drainpipes are often hard to see, it is not a good idea to let your ferret wander around an unknown area. Keep him on a leash!

for expansion, this more or less defeats the purpose because it makes the collar too easy to slip off.

Your pet's collar should be tight enough so that it does not easily slip off over his head but loose enough that with some effort you can get your little finger underneath it. You will probably have to punch extra holes in the collar in order to be able to adjust it properly. Remember to check a growing animal frequently to make sure the collar has not become too snug. Even a small weight gain in an adult animal can cause a collar

to be too tight. Be sure to have a spare collar and be prepared to replace lost collars several times a year, as most ferrets seem to manage to get out of them occasionally.

I suppose there is always some danger that a ferret may get hung up somewhere by his collar, but I feel that the dangers of not wearing a collar are much greater. Thus far I know of many ferret owners who have had their pet saved or returned because of the collar, but I still don't know of a single ferret that has had any problems caused by his collar.

CHEWING

While ferrets don't go through a destructive stage of chewing on things like most puppies do, they all seem to have a strange taste for sponges and the spongy material such as the kind the solid rubber play balls are made of. If given the chance, many ferrets will chew on and eat rubber toys, which can block up their intestines and result in death. Care should be taken to keep all dangerous toys and sponges out of reach of ferrets—sponges kept under the sink seem to be especially popular with and easily located by most ferrets.

Ferrets are also extremely fond of the hollow rubber squeak toys made for dogs and cats. They enjoy chewing on these toys, and many

An **ID** tag will identify your ferret as a pet, and it may get a lost ferret returned to you.

117

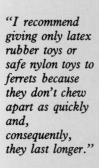

will chew until they have eaten a hole in the rubber. Not infrequently they will also swallow little bits and pieces of thin rubber, which usually, because they are very thin, pass through the digestive tract without causing trouble. Just to be on the safe side, though, it is still best to replace the toy when your pet has chewed it enough to eat a hole in it, as this material could possibly cause an intestinal obstruction. I recommend giving only latex rubber toys or safe nylon toys to ferrets because they don't chew apart as quickly and, consequently, they last longer.

ELECTRICAL WIRES

Most ferrets will not chew on the standard type of electrical cords and wires, but lots of them love to play with the coiled cord that connects the body of the telephone to the receiver. I assume the thing that makes it so much fun is that it offers some resistance and fights back

when they take it in their mouths and try to run away with it. I've come home several times to find the handset to the phone under the sofa—where my ferrets stashed it with their other toys when they finally got tired of dragging it around! Although I've never known a ferret that was injured from biting a telephone cord, I do know that if they play with it long enough the wires inside get broken and the phone won't work any more. If it is leased equipment and the phone company finds out why it doesn't work, they make you pay for replacing it! Some ferret owners report that they have been able to break their pet of the habit of playing with the receiver by spraying the cord with Bitter Apple (a foul tasting preparation available at pet stores).

POISONS

Poisons are a hazard for all pets (and small children, too) and should

Sponge balls are fun for ferrets but are very dangerous, as ferrets tend to eat objects made of this material.

Whenever you bathe your ferret, whether out of necessity or for a play session with a pal, be sure to supervise at all times.

be kept safely out of reach. If you are going to use roach poisons or any type of exterminating service, be sure to read the labels first or check with the exterminating company to make sure that these chemicals are safe to use with ferrets in the house. I find that boric acid is very safe and effective for getting rid of cockroaches, and it has the additional advantage of being relatively inexpensive. It is not harmful to small animals or children, but is quite toxic to roaches. It comes in a powder and can easily be sprinkled in cracks or crevices or other areas that harbor roaches.

FALLING

Falls are another hazard for ferrets. They are not surefooted like cats, and while they can often tolerate a fall of a great distance, because of their light weight they can also land in a bad position. A short fall of as little as four or five feet onto a hard surface can sometimes be fatal. It is a good idea to keep all windows screened (even if you think your pet can't climb up to the window) in rooms where your ferret will be running free—especially if they are above the ground floor. I learned this the hard way when one poor unfortunate young kit in my house

learned to climb up onto the windowsill one day and took a nosedive down four stories onto the concrete below. Luckily he survived, sustaining only a few broken ribs and a pneumothorax from a punctured lung, but it was undoubtedly a very painful experience for him and could have been avoided had I taken the proper precautions.

FREEDOM

Your ferret should not be allowed to run free outdoors unless you are watching him at all times. Once ferrets have gotten used to other animals, they will not be afraid, and they'll have no protection against a vicious dog or any other predator. In addition, while at first they will probably stay close to the house, they may eventually wander off and may easily get into trouble or get lost. If you are playing with your ferret in the park or in your yard, you may want to attach a leash to his collar and let him drag it around behind him. It will be useful for stopping him quickly when a strange dog approaches (or when he approaches a strange dog) or when he starts to disappear down a hole you hadn't noticed.

A group of 37-day-old ferrets. Note the differences in coat colors.

Where ferrets are concerned, an ounce of prevention is worth three pounds of cure since a ferret will explore anything and everything that is accessible to him.

TRAVELING WITH YOUR FERRET

"Another advantage of a carrier is that it provides confinement for automobile travel. Ferrets should not be allowed to run loose in an automobile, especially when it is moving, because they can be a dangerous distraction to the driver."

Because of their small size and easygoing natures, traveling with ferrets can be fun. For many years I took Melinda and McGuinn (and later Sally) with me wherever I went, both in and out of town. I found it most convenient to carry them in my shoulder bag, which held the ferrets and their bed and litter pan as well as serving as my purse, and sometimes my bookbag.

Because they would not jump down from any height, I found that I could keep them out of trouble by hanging their bag across the top of a door. At times when it was not convenient to keep them in a shower stall or bath tub, this served as their temporary area of confinement and they spent the many a night in their mobile home, hanging from the top of a door at a friend's house or in a motel room.

PORTABLE PENS

Another method I found for keeping them from running around and getting lost or into trouble in other people's houses was to put them on a leash and tie the end of it to their mobile home. This way they could explore the immediate area and still not be free to go discover and crawl into a hole under the sink, remove the insoles from all the shoes in a nearby closet or dig up potted plants. For safety reasons I never left them unattended while hanging from a door because while they never jumped, they did, on rare occasions, fall. I also did not usually have them out of my sight for long while they were tied up, because of the danger of their becoming tangled in the leashes.

For the most part they didn't mind this kind of restriction on their freedom when we were away from home, because I generally took them on two or three long walks each day, which allowed them to get their fill of investigating new territory.

Other people I know who travel with their ferrets, but don't want to spend so much time "fooling around" with them, find that a large cat carrier (complete with litter pan and bed, of course) is good for both transporting their pets and providing living quarters once they arrive at their destination. They report that the most difficult part is attaching the water bottle to the inside of the carrier, which can, nevertheless, be done with a string, wire, and a little imagination. The water bottle must be removed during transportation, however, because the motion of the carrier usually causes it to leak.

CARS

One of the advantages of a carrier is that it's safe to go off and leave your ferret in it unattended—provided it is not left in a car with the windows rolled up. I know of many ferrets, as well as other animals, who have been left in the car for only a short while and consequently have died from becoming overheated, because of the greenhouse effect of the sun shining in through the glass. In the absence of good air circulation, the inside of the car can rapidly become hot enough to kill an animal, even when the temperature outside is not so hot as to be uncomfortable.

Another advantage of a carrier is that it provides confinement for automobile travel. Ferrets should not be allowed to run loose in an automobile, especially when it is moving, because they can be a dangerous distraction to the driver.

Traveling with ferrets can be fun if proper planning is done ahead of time.

Most of them seem to be attracted to the area right under the driver's feet, where numerous unfortunate accidents can occur, including the crushing of an unsuspecting ferret beneath the brake pedal. Ferrets are always good at finding holes you don't know about and as a result may end up under the hood with the motor, or even on the highway! I've also heard that it's no fun to have to remove the back seat of the car, after reaching your destination, when no amount of coaxing will bring your ferret out of the nice cozy little nest he's made for himself from the stuffing he so cleverly dug out of the seat!

Keeping your ferret confined to a carrier in an automobile has one major drawback for your ferret—he usually can't see where he's going and what's going on around him quite well enough to suit his taste! Some ferrets, who obviously either never heard about or weren't impressed with curiosity killing the cat, find this to be almost intolerable, and will go about trying to rectify things by attempting to dig a hole in the carrier through which they can exit. Unfortunately, a curious ferret can be extremely persistent at this activity, which I've heard can be more than a little irritating and annoying to the other occupants of the car. In fact, I know of several ferret owners who eventually had to give up traveling with their pets because they found that the perpetual, inescapable sound of little ferret claws scratching the floor of the carrier drove them absolutely crazy!

Many ferret owners who have had this problem and have not wanted to abandon the idea of traveling with their pets have called or written me to ask for advice. Merry Kahn of Mequoketa, Iowa, for example, recently wrote: "We are envious of your ability to travel in a car with your ferrets. Our ferrets do not travel well. We have a travel hutch for them which we use when taking them to the vet or to my parent's home on the other side of the state. We try to make this hutch comfortable with food, water, and soft towels, but they rattle on the bars like convicts in prison. If we let them out, they immediately head for the gas and brake pedals and the interior of the dashboard. If we keep them in the travel hutch, they don't settle down for a long time. Maybe some ferrets simply don't travel well. What do you suggest?"

The best approach, and the one which has thus far been successful in all cases tested, is to completely ignore your ferret when he scratches on the carrier. This, of course, is much easier said than done—especially if you are   in the car! Given time (and sometimes it takes a great deal of time!), even the most optimistic little critter will eventually decide he's undertaken the impossible in endeavoring to dig his way out and will eventually give up and stop trying. On the other hand, if you give up and let him out when he scratches, you will only reinforce his behavior and encourage him to scratch when he wants you to let him out. Like many other ferret training projects, the outcome depends on which wears out first, your nerves or the ferret's optimism!

On the occasions when I traveled with my ferrets in a car and I was not driving, I kept them on a leash and let them sit on my lap. This worked out fairly well once they finally figured out it was another place where they weren't allowed to get down. Like most dogs, they all enjoyed sticking their noses out the window. McGuinn especially seemed to like the wind in her face and for some odd reason it always had the effect of making her want to jump out of the window, which she would

As young ferrets continue to grow, they gradually become more active.

have readily done had I not been holding on to either her, her leash, or her collar. I assume this strange urge to jump out had something to do with the wind, because she never attempted to jump out the window unless the car was moving fast enough to cause a breeze to blow across her face!

PERMISSION

Taking the ferrets with me wherever I went was very simple and easy to do when I stayed in town. There were very few places in New York City that I frequented where

their presence was not allowed, or even welcomed, and because they were so used to traveling and sleeping in their mobile home, I found that they were easily smuggled into the places they weren't normally allowed to go, such as movie theaters and nightclubs. I simply zipped up my shoulder bag and they disappeared—not to be seen nor heard from for hours at a time. They were especially willing to disappear if I took them on a ten or 15-minute walk first, after which they were usually tired and ready for a nap.

Smuggling them onto buses, trains, and airplanes, however, was an entirely different story, and a great deal more difficult than smuggling the skunks had been. The train station and airport weren't part of my ferrets' daily routine and somehow they always knew that something different was happening. Being such curious animals, they insisted on seeing where we were going and would excitedly pace back and forth from one side of their bag to the other, taking in everything. Naturally, they didn't want to be denied the opportunity to enjoy their new environment. As you might easily guess, when I attempted to hide them by zipping them up in their bed, they protested by scratching at the inside of the bag, making enough racket to attract the attention of anyone who was not totally deaf and standing within 30

"Taking the ferrets with me wherever I went was very simple and easy to do when I stayed in town."

It is not a good idea to take young ferrets on long trips before they have been weaned.

125

Many pet ferrets travel well, while others scratch at their cage incessantly. Keep in mind that all ferrets are individuals.

". . . I had to go to the airport several hours before my scheduled departure time. This gave Melinda and McGuinn enough time to look around until they got bored, after which they would voluntarily go to sleep."

feet.

Unfortunately, I couldn't solve this problem by ignoring it, because even if they only persisted in scratching for a short while it was just long enough to announce their presence to everyone around me. This made smuggling them anywhere impossible. I could zip them up before we got to the airport and they would go right to sleep; however, this proved to be no help because they always woke up the moment we arrived at the airport and proceeded to dig at the sides of the bag.

In order to solve this problem, I had to go to the airport several hours before my scheduled departure time. This gave Melinda and McGuinn enough time to look around until they got bored, after which they would voluntarily go to sleep, allowing me to zip them up and carry on my innocent-looking shoulder bag.

Now all of this sounds simple enough; however, there were several complications. If you walk around the airport for an hour or two with two ferrets excitedly pacing back and forth in your handbag, they're bound to attract attention, and more than likely will be noticed by someone who's getting on the same plane and who could potentially blow the whistle on your secret cargo.

For this reason I had to be very careful about where in the airport I took the ferrets to get them bored. After gaining a little experience, I eventually devised a sequence of steps designed to bore them as quickly and happily as possible, and it was usually quite effective.

I started out by keeping them awake at home before I left, and I did not allow them to snooze en route to the airport, hoping that they would be ready for a nap sooner.

Next I took them some distance from the airport, put on their leashes, and let them walk around and investigate the area, usually a parking lot or nearby field. When they were tired of exploring, usually in 15 or 20 minutes, they would indicate that they were ready to get back in the bag by standing up with

A small Nylabone® pet pacifier may help keep your ferret occupied and quiet during the trip. Nylabones® are available at pet shops.

their front paws on my leg. At that point we were ready to proceed to the terminal building. More often than not, the best place for boring them was inside the ladies' room, where I would hang their bag on a hook inside one of the stalls. There really wasn't much for them to look at, and while it still had some of the same smell or feel of the airport, they quickly found it to be pretty boring (so did I!) and would usually opt for a nap within three or four minutes.

When I was sure that they were sleeping, I would zip them up and go on my way. By this time they were usually tired enough that they wouldn't wake up again until we were safely on the plane or train. However, if they did wake up, a quick trip back to the ladies' room was generally enough to put them right back to sleep.

HEALTH PAPERS

In those old days of ferret smuggling I was much younger and more energetic, and slightly crazier.

Now I find that if I have occasion to travel with ferrets, the easiest, most sane, and reasonable thing is book them on the flight legally and pay a small extra fare for them. Some airlines will allow one animal in the cabin of the plane on each flight, if the animal is confined to a carrier which will fit under the seat. Most also require a health certificate stating that the animal is in good health and free from contagious disease.

If you plan to travel with your ferret, it is a good idea to check with the various airlines quite some time in advance, as not all of them will allow an animal on board, and those that do may have differing regulations and requirements.

If you are planning a long trip with your ferret, it is advisable to check the wildlife laws of the areas you will be traveling through, as, unfortunately, there are presently some places in which ferrets are illegal. In some regions, your ferret can legally be confiscated and put to death—even if you are only visiting in the area for a few days!

"In some regions, your ferret can legally be confiscated and put to death—even if you are only visiting in the area for a few days!"

BECOMING A TWO-FERRET FAMILY

"In the long run . . . no other animal or human can play ferret games quite as well as another ferret."

Over the years I've gotten many calls from people wanting to know: "Is it all right to have just one ferret, or should I get two so they can keep each other company?; "Will just one ferret get lonely and be unhappy if he doesn't have another ferret for a companion?; "If I buy another ferret, is it best to purchase one of the same sex, or will they get along better if I get one of the opposite sex?"

Most ferrets are very amiable and outgoing and will readily make friends with and become attached to another family pet, such as a cat or dog, which can fill the role of a companion quite nicely. I know of numerous such duos that are happily devoted to one another. This kind of relationship, however, usually develops best if both ferret and family pet are introduced to each other at a young age. Some older animals, especially cats, who tend to be somewhat snobbish and standoffish, are not willing to be friends with a ferret.

People, too, can be fun friends for a ferret, especially if they're willing to spend time playing the games ferrets like, such as "wrestle" and "chase."

In the long run, however, no other animal or human can play ferret games quite as well as another ferret. While it is definitely not necessary to have more than one ferret, as an "only" ferret won't be unhappy, he will probably have more fun if he's got another ferret for a companion.

In some ways two ferrets are a little more trouble for you to take care of than just one. They're bound to want to go in opposite directions when you take them out for a walk; bath times take twice as long; the litter pan gets twice as dirty (if you're lucky!); and there's usually one left to dig in your potted plants when the other has lost interest. But, for the most part, it's just about as easy to care for two ferrets as it is to care for one. You can use the same size cage (until you add a third ferret), and since they're small, feeding two is not much more expensive than feeding just one.

BOYS AND GIRLS TOGETHER

When it comes to keeping different sex combinations together, I have not found that males get along any better with other males than with females, or females with females. The only exception to this comes when dealing with unaltered males. Unless they have grown up together, unaltered males will fight very seriously, even to the death of one or both of them. Even unaltered males who have grown up together may fight when they go into season. In addition, a recently altered full-grown male should not be put with an unaltered male or another recently altered male, as it takes time for the male sex hormone, testosterone, to be cleared from the body, and also quite some time before the effects of this hormone are totally dissipated.

Once you've decided to get two ferrets, you're left with the question (unless you already had a ferret) of whether to obtain them both at the same time or to get one and add another later. I find that the advantage to getting them separately is that there is a period of time during which you can focus all your attention on the first ferret and get to know him better as a result. In addition, if you add the second when the first is an adult, you'll have the pleasure of having another energetic, frenetic kit in the house for a few months. Most ferrets stay quite playful as they get older, but they usually calm down somewhat as adults, and there is definitely a difference in their energy level. In fact, many ferret owners actually welcome the time when their wild and crazy kit finally settles down and is willing to sit still and be held and begins to become more passively affectionate.

OLD VERSUS YOUNG

The major disadvantage of obtaining ferrets one at a time is that you may have a problem with the older ferret not accepting the new arrival—apparently the ferret version of sibling rivalry. This seems to be an extremely common problem, and I get a great many calls from ferret owners who want to know what to do about their older ferret, who doesn't seem in the least bit interested in having a ferret chum, and instead seems intent on attacking and biting the intruder. Much like a human child eventually overcomes the initial jealousy of a new baby brother or sister, this "ferret rivalry" will usually, in time, work itself out.

I added Melinda to the family when McGuinn was a year old, and

"The major disadvantage of obtaining ferrets one at a time is that you may have a problem with the older ferret not accepting the new arrival—apparently the ferret version of sibling rivalry."

Two ferrets are twice as fun as one. Ferrets are friendly creatures that love companionship

Generally, the individual personalities of the ferrets will be more of a factor than will their sexes when it comes to getting along.

"Eventually all three became friends, but neither Melinda nor McGuinn ever became nearly as close to Sally as they were to each other. . . ."

the two of them immediately hit it off. Without even so much as a hint of friction, they became the best of buddies. By the time I got Sally, who was a year old, Melinda was three and McGuinn was four. They both unequivocally hated her at first sight, and they appeared intent to kill her. For several months I kept them separated except when I was nearby and able to keep an eye on them, for fear Sally would get hurt. Melinda and McGuinn were continually biting her on the back of the neck, and while they never drew blood, I never found out how far it would go because I always rescued Sally. It was obvious that it certainly wasn't all in fun. This type of battling for status is normal, however, and I know of no cases of serious wounds to a new arrival.

After several months of pulling Melinda and McGuinn off their enemy's back, accompanied by severe scoldings and an occasional spanking, they finally seemed to realize that Sally had come to stay

and they gradually accepted her presence and lost interest in torturing her. Although they tolerated her, for several more months they would not allow her to come and sleep with them, and would bite at her and drive her away when she tried to join them.

Eventually all three became friends, but neither Melinda nor McGuinn ever became nearly as close to Sally as they were to each other, and even after McGuinn died, Melinda never became as attached to Sally, or any of the other ferrets for that matter, as she had been to McGuinn.

Keeping Sally separated from Melinda and McGuinn for those first few months was easy to do and just seemed to happen naturally, because whenever I went out I left Sally home and took the other two with me, and at night I kept Sally in the kitchen while Melinda and McGuinn were allowed to sleep in, or under, my bed. I think they would have gotten used to each other and made friends sooner, however, if I had left them all in the same room with Sally in a cage where they could see her but not get to her to bother her.

When ferret owners Sue and Walter Endicott, from Florida, called and told me that their nine-month-old ferret, Fred, was attacking Jake, the new kit they got to keep Fred company, I assured them that the situation was temporary, and I suggested that they keep Jake in a cage immediately adjacent to Fred's instead of trying to leave them together in the same cage.

For the first month they kept Jake caged all of the time (Fred was caged only at night), bringing him out several times a day to play with Fred. "We constantly monitored the boys' play," they told me, "admonishing Fred whenever we thought he was too rough. Jake was very vocal. His squeaks and squeals made it seem as though he was being trampled by Fred. We were always quick to come to Jake's rescue and so we were never sure, consequently, how much of our monitoring was really necessary. After about three weeks things had changed entirely and Fred and Jake became inseparable, as they still are today."

In a similar manner, all the older ferrets eventually worked through their differences with the new kits and all eventually became good friends in spite of the fact that when their very upset owners called me, they were afraid that it was never going to work out and that they were certain that they were going to have to get rid of their newest addition.

The longest period of adjustment I know of so far was about four months, but I have not yet heard of two ferrets (with the exception of two unaltered males or recently altered males) who will not eventually at least tolerate one another, if not become the best of friends.

HOW THEY DO IT IN PEORIA

Bonnie Hauck of Peoria, Illinois, wrote to tell me about her experiences in adding new ferrets to her family.

"We got our second ferret, a female we named Buggs, when Hooter (so named after my husband Jim's slang expression for a nosy person) was about six months old. Hooter was so excited I thought he would have a heart attack. He flung himself at the glass aquarium in which the new baby was housed. As soon as we placed the little one on the floor he immediately seized it by the nape of the neck and tried to drag it under the tea chest with his other toys. I feared for the little animal's safety since Hooter was so

rough, and we let them play together only under supervision for the next few days.

"Buggs entered our household with the slightest ripple of inconvenience. She ate and slept with Hooter and used his litter pan with little or no direction from us. They became inseparable buddies, and I still remember Hooter searching under furniture and in closets for hours when Buggs was away at the vet's being spayed. In personality, they were totally opposite. Hooter lies at my feet every morning in the bathroom while I put on my makeup and every evening in the kitchen while I make dinner. He will lie on his back in your arms like a baby while you scratch his ears. He can also hear you peel a banana in his sleep from two rooms away!

"Buggs is friendly and can be very playful but is more aloof and maintains a certain personal dignity at all times. While Hooter is a bit of

"The longest period of adjustment I know of so far was about four months, but I have not yet heard of two ferrets (with the exception of two unaltered males or recently altered males) who will not eventually at least tolerate one another, if not become the best of friends."

Even ferrets of different ages can become good friends.

a slob, Buggs is very neat and precise. She refuses to use a pan that is too dirty and looks at it with such disgust that I always rush to clean it up right away. She eats very slowly and often loses her treats to Hooter, who will gulp his down so that he can eat hers. When eating anything messy or wet she licks her whiskers after every bite. They both hide their toys, but Buggs has some that are always kept in particular places. If one is moved or if you are caught playing with it, she will politely but firmly take it away and put it in its proper place.

"Into this tranquil and harmonious setting came Inky, about a year later. Buggs was probably about two years old at this time and Hooter about two and a half. Inky was already as big as Buggs, but it was apparent she was still a youngster.

"She was quite lovable, and I was expecting my family to welcome the little waif with open arms when Buggs attacked with a ferocity that surprised me. I was also painfully reminded that she had never been descented. The spitting and squealing that followed was absolutely terrifying, and I had to swat Buggs several times before she would release her grip on the little tyke. Buggs was immediately locked in the large cage she shared with Hooter, and Inky's neck wounds

were liberally swabbed with peroxide. Hooter was interested but more restrained, since he was an old hand at new additions. Inky, however, was absolutely crazy about Hooter and immediately adopted him as her big brother. She still follows him everywhere, and it is easy to tell that this sometimes wears on Hooter, but he maintains as much dignity as possible while vainly trying to use the litter pan alone.

"Fortunately, we happened to have a large empty aquarium and set this up as Inky's temporary new home. For weeks my life revolved around rotating Inky and Buggs so that each could have a period of freedom without the other. When Buggs was loose I usually put Inky in the large cage, as it was roomier. Buggs spent most of her free time eating Inky's food and stealing Inky's toys and hissing at Inky through the cage bars. All during this time, however, Inky was growing larger and engaging in some vigorous rough-and-tumble sessions with Hooter, who was probably twice her weight.

"This went on for about three weeks before Jim had finally had enough and took on the job of supervising some daily sessions in which the three were let out together. We did this in a small room with no furniture so they couldn't

When introducing a new ferret to an older, more established one, it is wise to supervise their interactions at first.

fight where we could not reach them. Jim simply let them out together and at first just held Inky while Buggs sniffed at her. If Buggs bit her she was swatted. If she bit too hard she was confined to jail to watch Jim play with Inky. I believe that letting Inky use the big cage also helped to get her scent into Buggs's territory and helped Buggs get used to the idea more quickly. This process might have been speeded up if Inky was in a proper cage rather than an aquarium, but Jim was convinced that we would not work at negotiation nearly as hard if a permanent living arrangement was found. It may have been our efforts or just the fact that Inky was finally big enough to hold her own, but after three weeks of supervision, they worked out a truce. About six weeks after we had first brought Inky home we were able to let them all run free together. There was still some awful squealing, but we began to notice that no one was biting. There was shoulder bumping and bristling but no real damage. Finally, after we found them asleep together we began to let Inky 'sleep over' in the big cage, first for short nap sessions, then overnight.

"Inky has shown no ill effects and plays with Hooter and Buggs until they have had enough. No longer bullied, she has become 'Inky the Terrible' and is always into more mischief than the other two. She

climbs on top of our aquarium to drink the water and pull the floss out of the filter. She climbs up my stereo speakers to terrorize the lovebirds overhead. She nips at my wet feet when I try to step out of the shower, and hits the litter pans now and then only because they happen to be in corners. Still, there is something very lovable about her and it is difficult to stay angry at her when she comes dancing across the room in mock attack. She loves to be tickled and can always be made to yawn by scratching her ears just so. She also can make me laugh after the toughest day."

If you exercise patience when introducing ferrets to one another, it is very likely that they will at least tolerate each other and will probably become good friends.

" '. . . Jim was convinced that we would not work at negotiation nearly as hard if a permanent living arrangement was found.' "

FERRETS AND OTHER ANIMALS

"The more it runs away, the more fun it is to chase, and if it makes noise when they tease it, the game is even more enjoyable."

Ferrets are generally very amiable creatures, and most of them are compatible with both dogs and cats as well as numerous other household pets. They readily form friendships with, and attachments to, other animals and will wrestle and play "chase" with dogs, cats, and sometimes even skunks and rabbits.

My ferrets seem to have one general rule of thumb when it comes to dealing with other animals. If it fights back when they good-naturedly attack it and seems very serious about the whole thing, they wisely leave it alone and give it a wide berth when it's necessary for them to be in close proximity. If it fights back rather halfheartedly, they consider it a potential playmate, and usually after a brief period of adjustment on the part of the animal in question, they eventually become good friends and engage in raucous wrestling matches and games of chase and "hit and run." On the other hand, if an animal is frightened or annoyed by the ferrets without seeming terribly threatening to them, they will tease, bother, and worry it relentlessly. The more it runs away, the more fun it is to chase, and if it makes noise when they tease it, the game is even more enjoyable!

FERRETS AND DOGS

My ferrets like dogs and have several dog friends they play with, while my cats are terrified and keep a good distance between themselves and all dogs, both large and small.

When McGuinn was very young she had a German Shepherd friend who would carry her around in his mouth. She would come up to him and nip at his heels and then run away and he would chase her. When he finally managed to catch her, he would pick her up and carry her around in his mouth. When he put her down she would lie on her back and nip at his nose while kicking at him with her back feet; then she'd get up and run under the sofa where he couldn't reach her. When his back was turned she'd run out and make a flying leap at his tail, take a quick nip, and run for cover. When he finally managed to catch her, he'd walk around the house again with McGuinn calmly dangling from his mouth. After a while he'd drop the very damp little ferret and she'd go for his nose again and the chase would be on.

This particular dog had cat friends that he played with in the same manner, so it was perhaps for this reason that he wasn't frightened of McGuinn when he first met her. Many dogs, however, and many cats as well, are frightened, or at least appreciably apprehensive, when first coming face to face with a ferret. Most ferrets, even those who have never seen a cat or dog before, will fearlessly run right up and want to play. They seem to think that everything is made to have fun with and nothing is going to hurt them. To an animal who has never seen one, a ferret has a strange, unfamiliar appearance and odor, and the bold manner in which a ferret is likely to approach is often quite disconcerting and frightening. After all, most dogs and cats are used to other little creatures being frightened of them and running away. No squirrel, for example, is just going to stand around nonchalantly and let a dog or cat walk over to meet him. When the tables are turned and a small ferret

Since ferrets love to play, they usually get along with most larger animals; in addition, they especially like children.

walks (or runs) right up, possibly even taking a playful nip at a nose, paw, or tail, the approached animals are unsure about the ferret's intentions and about what is going to happen next, and they frequently respond with fear by running away.

FERRETS AND CATS

When I was working my way through undergraduate school, one of the ways I earned money for tuition was by boarding cats, and many an owner would drop a cat off at my house with the warning: "Be careful about letting my cat around your ferrets—she catches and kills chipmunks and rabbits in the woods. I'd hate to come back and find that she's killed one of your little pets." It was usually those same killer cats that were absolutely terrified and ran away from the ferrets. After all, how can you chase it if it won't run away? I suppose it's reasonable to assume that those same cats would be just as terrified if they were suddenly attacked by a chipmunk one day while strolling through the woods.

Although most dogs and cats get along well with ferrets once they overcome their initial fear, you should keep in mind that all dogs and cats are capable of injuring or killing a ferret, and some that do not like ferrets will readily do so, especially hunting breeds. You should never allow your ferret to approach a strange dog or cat because he cannot protect himself against an attack, and one bite could easily end his life. When introducing your pet ferret to a dog or cat, it is best to do so gradually, holding him in such a manner that your hands will protect him from an unexpected bite. Let the dog or cat sniff him and watch the reaction. I think that it probably helps the dog or cat to view a ferret as a potential friend rather than something to be attacked when they see you hold, pet, and talk to it—although your own dogs or cats may react with jealousy. When you feel fairly confident that the dog or cat will not hurt the ferret, you may let him down, but it is best to stay close to the ferret at first, so you can pick him up quickly should the dog or cat give any indication that he is going to bite your pet. Even when you think the animals are going to get along, you should not let them play together without being there to

No matter what type of animal you introduce to your ferret, a proper period of supervision is necessary.

136

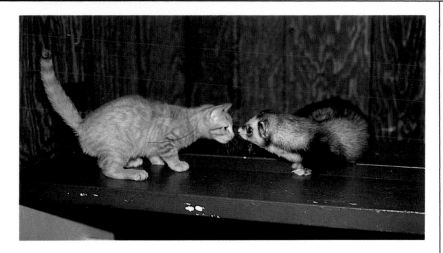

watch for the first few times. Only when they have established a friendship and routine of play is it safe to leave them together unsupervised.

Special caution should be used when introducing a ferret to terriers, which have been bred to be ratters, as these breeds, more than others, are likely to kill a ferret.

Some people have expressed concern that a pet ferret will kill their dog or cat. This is next to, if not entirely, impossible, and I have never heard of a pet ferret inflicting a really serious injury on a dog or cat, much less killing one.

I do know of a three-year-old ferret, Rocky, who recently bit the family cat, Roscoe, at the base of the tail, causing an abscess to form and necessitating a trip to the local vet. It was the first time Rocky had ever broken the cat's skin, although in the two years that the pair have known each other Rocky has taken every available opportunity to attack and bite Roscoe, a three-year-old male tabby. As you might suspect, Roscoe hates Rocky and is very careful to steer clear of the pesky "varmint." On the other hand, Roscoe and Sophie, the younger ferret member of the family, are the best of friends and spend hours together wrestling and chasing one another around the house. Their owner, Tim Anderson of Cincinnati,

Ohio, isn't quite sure if Rocky really dislikes the cat or just "enjoys deviling him and giving him a hard time," but he is certain that Roscoe, who weighs over ten pounds, could easily maim or kill his little tormentor if he chose to fight rather than to run away.

The only circumstance in which it is feasible that a ferret could kill a dog or cat would be if the dog or cat were sick or injured and unconscious; even then it is highly unlikely that a pet ferret would have any desire to kill a comatose dog or cat— or any dog or cat for that matter. The one exception to this might possibly be newborn kittens or puppies, and it is advisable to make such infant animals inaccessible to ferrets until they are old enough to run away if need be.

FEAR

Most ferrets have no fear of a dog unless they've been previously injured by one. I have known ferrets, however, that were unusual in that they were absolutely terrified of all dogs. My friend David's ferret, Possum, would not go near a dog and would scream in panic if one came near her. She never had any bad experiences with dogs that we know of, and just seems to have been born that way. She screamed the very first time she met a dog—and he was a little dog at that!

I have not yet heard of a ferret that's afraid of cats, unless it's been chased and hurt by one, but I'm sure there are probably some somewhere that I will hear about sooner or later!

My ferrets like cats and enjoy teasing BoJeangles, my Siamese cat who is now in her late teens. She is very good natured and has been taught that she is not to hurt any of the baby bunnies, squirrels, ferrets, skunks, weasels, birds, or other miscellaneous animals that have passed through my kitchen for one reason or another. In fact, BoJeangles has learned that lesson so well that, like Roscoe, she won't fight back when the ferrets jump her and nip at her ears, paws, and tail. Instead, she just yowls loudly (as only a Siamese can!) and runs away—usually with one or more of the ferrets hot on her heels. Sometimes they chase her all over the house for as long as ten minutes, so she generally considers them pests to be tolerated. On those extremely rare occasions when she does condescend to play with them, it is usually from the top of a chair where they can't reach her but she can reach down and bat at them with her paws. The ferrets love this game and

jump at her, trying to nip her foot as she swipes down at them.

I felt sorry for BoJeangles because she was so tolerant of the ferrets and yet not really friendly with them, so I decided to get her a friend that she would really like, another cat.

When I got Brienza, who is a chocolate point Siamese, she was only six weeks old and a very tiny kitten. I had to protect her from the ferrets, who wanted to jump on her and bite her—Moseley, to play, and Melinda, who seemed to be jealous and appeared to want to hurt her. Brienza was overwhelmed by the ferrets and understandably didn't like them too well. In three or four weeks, however, she grew bigger and things began to change. She was no longer overpowered by the ferrets and began to enjoy playing with them. She would hide or get up on a chair or table and ambush them when they passed by. Soon it would turn into a wrestling match and they would play together, kicking and biting at each other and rolling around on the floor together much the same as two kittens or puppies would. First I'd hear Brienza cry because a ferret would get too rough and bite or kick too hard, and then I'd hear a ferret cry because the kitten had gotten too rough. BoJeangles, being old and not as

Some cats and ferrets become so friendly with each other that they share their food and sleep together.

Ferrets will generally get along best with cats that are introduced when kittens, as older cats are usually not as playful.

playful as the ferrets, would occasionally play with Brienza, but the ferrets (except Melinda, who gave up attacking Brienza once she got big enough to fight back but still didn't like her) were always ready and willing to play with her; consequently, she was crazy about them and continued to be crazy about them as she got older and bigger. Now that she is a full grown cat, she still likes the ferrets so much that she will sit on top of or lie next to their cage if for some reason I have them locked up. Brienza's best friend is Melinda's grandson and Sally's son, Christopher, who is five months younger than she is and who, because he is young, will play with her longer than the other ferrets will without tiring. They chase each other all through the house and stalk and jump each other and generally get very rowdy—so rowdy that it is sometimes necessary to lock one or both of them up because they make so much racket that it is impossible to sleep through it all. Moseley and Sally play with Brienza, but for shorter periods of time. Melinda, who is sick and weak and sleeps most of the time, won't play at all, and I have to protect her from Brienza, who occasionally pounces on her, wanting to start a wrestling match.

SKUNKS

Most ferrets enjoy teasing other animals. Melinda and McGuinn used to enjoy teasing my two skunks, Eli and Elliot, which they did by chasing them around the apartment, leaping over them and onto their backs while trying to hold on. Elliot would not put up with such nonsense and usually got out of the game soon after it started by giving a ferret or two a good bite—not hard enough to break the skin or draw blood but hard enough to convince the ferrets that he was no fun at all. Eli was less aggressive about fighting them off, and sometimes they could get a skunk-back ride from him. He usually squealed as he ran along trying to shake them off his back, making it all the more fun for the ferrets. Eli, too, however, would eventually stand his ground and stomp, hiss, and bite the ferrets until they were finally convinced that he meant serious business. At this point the ferrets would back down and go off in search of another form of amusement.

In general the skunks weren't especially crazy about the ferrets, but on rare occasions they would allow the ferrets to come and join them for a snooze, usually when they were already asleep in their bed. The skunks would wake up briefly when

"Most ferrets enjoy teasing other animals. Melinda and McGuinn used to enjoy teasing my two skunks, Eli and Elliot, which they did by chasing them around the apartment, leaping over them and onto their backs while trying to hold on."

Ferrets and skunks are both members of the family Mustelidae. Although the coloration of skunks is more striking, their personalities are less playful than those of their ferret cousins.

a ferret or ferrets got in, and then, possibly deciding that moving to another bed wasn't worth the effort, would go back to sleep. In this same manner Sally would occasionally join BoJeangles for a nap. This was rare, however, because all the ferrets were much more likely to jump on and nip a sleeping skunk or cat than they were to crawl in and go to sleep.

GUINEA PIGS

I haven't heard too much about how ferrets and guinea pigs get along, but I have had one experience with this combination. One evening I brought into my apartment a guinea pig that some of the neighborhood kids had thoughtfully abandoned on my doorstep. It didn't take Melinda long to discover that the guinea pig was deathly afraid of her, so naturally she jumped on its back and held onto its left ear while it ran crazily around the room in utter panic. It was screaming at the top of its lungs and sounded like it thought the end was near. I wasn't so sure myself that the end wasn't near at hand, because the guinea pig was so terrified that I was afraid it was going to have a heart attack and drop dead before I could apprehend the two of them and stop Melinda from torturing it. I doubt that Melinda would really have hurt it (she never hurt Eli), but the poor little pig didn't know that.

"My ferrets aren't allowed to play with guinea pigs any more because I really don't think that they mix too well. I would also advise against trying to mix white mice, hamsters, or gerbils with ferrets. . . ."

Fortunately, I was finally able to pluck Melinda from its back as it ran by me and I was later able to find it a good home with a nice little boy in a ferretless family.

My ferrets aren't allowed to play with guinea pigs any more because I really don't think that they mix too well. I would also advise against trying to mix white mice, hamsters, or gerbils with ferrets, as it is quite possible that such a small animal would end up seriously injured or dead and a few ferrets, who are among the less finicky eaters, might even be willing to try a taste or two of such a creature.

FROGS

Melinda had fun playing with a frog one day in my biology class. She repeatedly chased it, caught it, and let it go until she broke its leg, at which time she abandoned it because it was no longer any fun when it didn't hop. Although I don't think she intended to hurt the frog, she played too rough and consequently she, and all my other ferrets for that matter, are no longer allowed to play with frogs.

RABBITS

There are also some rabbits who are terrified of ferrets and who my ferrets would love to chase and tease if I let them. On the other hand, my friend Mary Bloom had a young male lop-eared rabbit named

Barnaby who was larger than the ferrets but of the same size or smaller than other rabbits they would tease if given the chance. Barnaby, however, was a bold, fearless, and downright tough rabbit, and he wasn't in the least frightened by ferrets. Melinda and McGuinn were quite surprised one day, while we were visiting Mary, when Barnaby chased and bit them. After that they were both afraid to even go near him.

Ferrets and rabbits can be friends, however, and I know of several families where ferrets share a cage and/or sleeping quarters with rabbits and they all live together quite peaceably. In any case, care should be taken when introducing a ferret to a rabbit or any other small helpless animal, as I am sure that there are some ferrets who might hurt or even kill a smaller animal if the opportunity presented itself.

BIRDS

Melinda and McGuinn tried to kill another creature only one time; that was a bird and it was under unusual circumstances. It was at a time when my apartment was being renovated, so for several months I moved into the guest bedroom belonging to a veterinarian friend of mine. As it turned out, the guest room was also

the parrot's room. I wasn't sure how my ferrets would react to the bird, so I kept them in a cage most of the time; I let them out to play several times a day when I was there to supervise. At first the ferrets showed no interest whatsoever in the parrot—they totally ignored it, almost as if it didn't exist. The bird, however, was extremely fascinated by the ferrets and would walk as close as 16 or 18 inches from them to investigate. Melinda and McGuinn were both usually very curious about everything, including other animals, but for some reason they just didn't pay any attention to the parrot, even when he walked near them.

Late one afternoon, after a few days of ferret-watching, the bird climbed up the side of the ferret cage and began walking about on the top of it, squawking at the ferrets. After five or six minutes the parrot finally got McGuinn so annoyed that she grabbed, in her mouth, the part of the parrot's foot that was sticking through into the cage and would not let go. The bird struggled and squawked until I finally opened the cage and released him from McGuinn's jaws. The poor parrot went away squawking, but in less than 15 minutes he was back on top of the cage again with his foot in a ferret's mouth, screeching loudly

". . . care should be taken when introducing a ferret to a rabbit or any other helpless animal, as I am sure that there are some ferrets who might hurt or even kill a smaller animal if the opportunity presented itself."

Three members of the author's unusual menagerie: a ferret, a cat, and a skunk.

and struggling to get away. I set him free again and no sooner was he rescued than he was back up on top of the cage, caught again. After about the fifth or sixth time, I decided things had gone far enough and that if I didn't do something to interrupt this foolish game, I'd end up having to bring a bird with a broken foot or leg downstairs to the doctor's office. I covered the cage with a sheet so that the parrot couldn't tease the ferrets any more— or so I thought! But the bird was amazingly persistent and managed to get under the sheet and on top of the cage again, squawking as usual. Once again a ferret grabbed him by the foot and once again I intervened and set him free. In less than ten minutes he was back under the sheet. I rescued him yet another time and then, using safety pins, I fastened the sheet to the top and sides of the cage so that the parrot couldn't get underneath it. This finally ended his silly game.

About half an hour later, my friend the veterinarian came upstairs and suggested that I let the ferrets out of the cage so he could watch them play. I opened the cage door. Melinda and McGuinn began to jump around crazily, as only ferrets at play can. Melinda pounced upon McGuinn and a wrestling match began. Just then the parrot became interested and started walking toward them. He was about 18 inches from them when they noticed him, and almost before I realized what was happening, they simultaneously leapt upon him. He screeched frantically and both the doctor and I made a mad dive for the tangle of feathers and fur. I reached in and pulled Melinda out of the pile. She had a long green feather hanging out of one side of her mouth. A split second later my friend yelled, "Ouch, she bit me!" and jerked his hand back. I handed

him Melinda to hold and then stuck my hand into the squawking pile again and withdrew it with McGuinn, who was struggling wildly. "She bit me!" the doctor repeated, waving his bleeding finger in front of my face. I explained that I didn't think she really meant to bite him, but had merely been caught up in the frenzy of the moment and was crazily biting at everything.

The bird, too, was bleeding, but both of them survived the ordeal essentially unharmed. While my friend still likes to watch the ferrets play, the parrot, understandably, lost all interest in ferret-watching as well as ferret-teasing.

CHICKENS

Once when McGuinn was about a year old I decided to see if ferrets could get along with chickens. I was visiting my friends Roger and Linda McGuinn in Malibu, California. They happened to be keeping a flock of chickens at the time, and naturally I was curious about how McGuinn would react to meeting the birds (not the Byrds!). Early one morning I took her out to the chicken yard with me when I went to gather the eggs, and I held her right up in front of a big hen's face. She immediately turned her head to the side and refused to look at the chicken—and no matter which way I turned her she continued to turn her head away from the chicken. I finally gave up and put her down on the ground, thinking maybe she might be willing to walk up to one and meet it on her own. I watched her carefully because I wasn't entirely certain that she wouldn't attack one of the birds, even though they were all much larger. I needn't have worried, though, because

Ferrets have been known to gang up on other animals and tease them; therefore, if you have an older, slower cat, dog, or other pet, you may wish to keep him away from your frisky ferrets.

". . . at one point the parakeet actually went over and regurgitated food for the baby ferret, just as though it were feeding a baby parakeet of its own!"

McGuinn just sniffed around the ground for a few seconds and then immediately began digging a hole in the chicken yard, ignoring all of the chickens. She dug for at least five minutes without even appearing to notice a chicken, so I finally took her back into the house.

PARAKEETS

I'm not sure how well the average ferret mixes with the average bird, but my friend Chuck Morton recently told me this interesting story.

"I'm certainly skeptical of some of the tales that ferret owners tell, so when this fellow who had recently purchased a ferret from me started telling me this wonderful story about how it gets along with his parakeet, I took it with several grains of salt and dismissed it as another exaggeration. Several weeks later I had the occasion to be at his house on an unrelated matter and was sort of surprised to notice that as soon as I started to approach the baby ferret, which was about eight or nine weeks old by then, the parakeet came over, flapping its wings and screeching at me in an obvious attempt to drive me away from the ferret. When I sat down and put the ferret in my lap, the parakeet flew over and stayed out of reach of my hand, but landed on the outside part of my lap, and it certainly appeared as if he was

prepared to guard the ferret and make sure I didn't hurt it. As soon as I put the ferret down, the parakeet immediately flew away from me and wouldn't allow me to come within ten feet of him. Whenever I picked up the ferret, however, the parakeet would come flying back and land on my lap—it seemed as though to protect the ferret. I watched these two animals play together on the floor, and I've never seen such a strange bond as they seemed to have between them. First the ferret would chase the little parakeet for awhile, and then the parakeet would chase the ferret!

"Well, obviously at this point I began to believe a lot more in the parakeet/ferret story that the fellow had told me. He said that the parakeet would take its seed and go over and put it in the ferret's cage. The cage was made of one by two-inch wire, so the parakeet could slip into the cage with the ferret and play with it, and peck at it and groom and preen it; the parakeet seemed to have adopted the ferret. He also said that at one point the parakeet actually went over and regurgitated food for the baby ferret, just as though it were feeding a baby parakeet of its own! The kicker to the story is that for years the fellow had a hamster in the same room as the bird—and the bird totally ignored it!"

HORSES

I know of a ferret that lives on a farm in Georgia who used to like to chase the horses. He'd go out to the pasture, walk up to a particular horse, and nip its foot. The horse was afraid and would run from the ferret—which made it great fun for the ferret! Unfortunately, one day the horse changed the rules of the game and, instead of running away, stepped on the surprised little ferret and broke its back. The ferret subsequently recovered, but has never gone back to the horse pasture to play!

The only other time I know of a ferret and horse interacting was when I had McGuinn, Melinda, and Eli (the skunk) on the terrace of a penthouse in New York City for a photographic session. They were to be in a photograph on the cover of *New York Magazine* along with a lovely lady model, a rabbit, and a Shetland pony. Getting the animals to stand still and stay in their assigned places all at the same time was a chore to tax the patience of even the best animal photographer, and the session dragged on and on all afternoon. During one of the many breaks, I placed Melinda on the pony's back, curious to see what she would do. She sniffed him for a few seconds, walked up his neck, sat on his head, and, quite predictably, nipped him on the ear! The pony started, whinnied, and gave its head a shake. I caught Melinda just as she was thrown off, and yes, you guessed it—my ferrets are no longer allowed to play with horses!

Ferrets often show affection toward one another. How that affection is received depends on the recipient ferret's personality.

". . . I placed Melinda on the pony's back, curious to see what she would do. She sniffed him for a few seconds, walked up his neck, sat on his head, and, quite predictably, nipped him on the ear!"

How friendly
particular
ferrets become
with other
animals in the
house depends
on the
individual
ferret
personality
and that of the
other pet in
question.

FERRET LESSONS

"*Ferrets, unlike cats, are not easily frightened and are not likely to bolt and run in a blind panic if dropped in the middle of an unfamiliar situation.*"

Ferrets love meeting people and going to new places, so I frequently take two or three of them with me wherever I go. People are always amazed at how "well behaved" they are. Numerous readers of my books have called and asked me the method I used to train them, and I explain that training a ferret to sit quietly on your lap and be well behaved is really more a matter of taking advantage of the ferret's innate personality than it is of instructing them, and it is usually quite easily accomplished.

Ferrets, unlike cats, are not easily frightened and are not likely to bolt

In a new situation, the ferret's first desire is to satisfy its curiosity by exploring.

and run in a blind panic if dropped in the middle of an unfamiliar situation. For example, to try to carry almost any cat in your arms out on the street if he's never been outside before (and sometimes even if he has) is sheer folly. You'll probably get scratched to start with, and if you put the cat down on the ground, in all likelihood he'll be so frightened that he'll run away, very fast, without bothering to look or consider where he's going. In addition, he may not stop running, and catching him again may prove to be very difficult, if not impossible.

Ferrets, on the other hand, don't seem to be nearly as frightened by unfamiliar surroundings, and the average ferret, when put down on the ground in a strange place, seems to have the good sense to stand still and look around a few seconds before determining in which direction to go to get to safety. Getting to safety usually entails walking, not running, to the nearest wall, or if a wall is not available, to the nearest bush or tree. Catching him again usually involves no more than walking over to him and picking him up—unless, of course, he has happened to find a hole to crawl down, in which case retrieving him can be quite difficult!

In addition to being basically calm, easygoing, and sensible animals, ferrets are generally intelligent, amiable, and are willing to accept whatever situation they might find themselves in, once they have determined to their satisfaction that the situation definitely can't be changed. Hence the secret of teaching a ferret to sit on your lap while you sit on a bus, in the subway, in a classroom, or at a friend's house is to convince him that you definitely aren't going to let him get down off your lap, and that it's a situation that's not going to change.

Young ferrets are usually more curious and active than older ones, but sometimes an older ferret can set an example for the youngster.

COLLAR AND LEASH

Getting this point across is simply a matter of using physical restraint to make it impossible for him to get off your lap. This is most easily done if he is wearing a collar, either with or without an attached leash. Hold your ferret in such a manner that whenever he tries to move he can go no further than a few steps in each direction. Initially you can expect him to put up quite a struggle. How long this little battle between you and your pet goes on depends on the personality of your particular ferret. Some ferrets are more persistent and less willing to give up than others. Ferrets who are young or especially curious, as well as bold and brave, may put up more of a fight than an older ferret or one who tends to be a little cautious and timid about exploring a new environment.

Regardless of how long the struggle continues, it is of primary importance that you win and your ferret loses and stops trying to get down. Then you can let go of his collar and allow him to move around—and each time he goes too far and starts to get off your lap, grab his collar or otherwise restrain him again and hold onto him until he stops struggling. He will probably learn the rules most quickly if you expose him to the same situation several times a day for several days in a row. Most ferrets have good memories, and after being in the same room at a friend's house every day for a week, your ferret will recognize the room and remember it as a place where he has tried unsuccessfully to get off your lap— and rather than bother to expend any effort to fight a losing battle he will eventually be content to sit on your lap and look around.

Once the novelty of the situation wears off, you may find that your ferret will only want to look around for a few minutes, and then will get

bored and fall asleep in your lap— and there you have it, a trained ferret! Probably the hardest part of the whole training procedure is having to feel like a cruel and mean monster when initially restraining the poor little critter on your lap.

I found that once the point was made and the rules had been laid down, neither Melinda nor McGuinn ever tried to get off my lap—as long as the situation was an old one. In a new place there was usually a brief test to see what the rules were going to be.

For example, I usually took both Melinda and McGuinn to school with me every day, and it was understood in no uncertain terms that they weren't allowed to get down and walk around in the classroom. This was no problem until the beginning of a new semester when we went to a new and different classroom. For the first two or three days in a new room, Melinda would always try to get off my lap. (McGuinn wasn't quite as curious or eager to explore and usually wouldn't bother.) Melinda, having been through these arguments with me before, seldom persisted in trying to get down longer that 30 or 40 seconds before realizing that this room, just like the rest, was going to be another one of those boring places where there was nothing to do except take a nap on my lap. She'd try two or three days in a row just to make absolutely certain, and then after that we'd never have any arguments about her behavior in that particular room again. I always found it somewhat amazing that she could tell the difference between one classroom and another since they all looked so much the same to me!

There was only one exception to this longstanding pattern, and it occurred because one day in the middle of the semester I went to

Ferrets love to
have fun and
are not afraid
of new places,
situations, or
objects.

Teaching a ferret to sit quietly on your lap means physically keeping him there until he loses the desire to continue struggling.

"After the first week of riding on a bus or subway, I never had any arguments with either Melinda or McGuinn about the rules unless someone sat down next to us with a shopping bag. . . ."

According to the author, it is the ferret on the leash that trains the owner to follow after him, rather than the ferret himself becoming leash trained.

chemistry class ten minutes early and allowed one of my classmates to walk Melinda around the room on her leash. Melinda was delighted to finally be allowed to investigate, and the next time we went into that particular classroom we had a two or three-minute battle about whether or not she was going to get down and run around on the floor again. If ferrets could talk, I'm sure Melinda would have said, "But why can't I get down? I got to get down the other day!" We argued for the next three class periods held in that classroom before she finally gave up the hope of being allowed to get down again.

After the first week of riding on the bus or subway, I never had any arguments with either Melinda or McGuinn about the rules unless someone sat down next to us with a shopping bag—in which case they both wanted to get in the bag and look around so badly that they'd occasionally try to see if they could get away with it. Usually they couldn't!

OUTDOOR TRAINING

Over the years many ferret owners have contacted me to ask if I can tell them how to leash-train their ferrets. Unfortunately, I was never able to teach any of my ferrets to walk along at my side—either with or without being on a leash. They, on the other hand, were finally successful in training me to follow along behind them wherever they chose to go when I had them attached to a leash.

Many times on cold days, when I put a leash on McGuinn and placed her down on the ground, she would follow along, running close behind me when I walked at a brisk pace. To the casual observer she certainly looked leash-trained; however, if I slowed down or stopped she would run up to me, place both of her little front paws on my leg, and gaze up at me longingly. This was her way of imploring me to pick her up so she could get back inside her nice warm mobile home. Instead of being leash-trained she was simply trying to

catch up with me so she could be carried, which she usually preferred to walking around, even when it wasn't cold outside. On those occasions when she did want to be down on the ground, she clearly had no interest in going where I was going and always wanted to head off in whichever direction particularly appealed to her at the time—usually dictated by her curiosity. As far as I know, this desire to choose their own direction and explore areas that especially attract their attention is typical of most ferrets, and I have not yet heard of anyone who has had any success in leash-training their ferret.

COME

Like many animals, ferrets can be taught to come when called—and will do so most of the time. In this respect they seem to fall somewhere between dogs, who generally always come when you call them, and cats, who come only if they are in the mood.

To teach your ferret to come when called, begin by repeating his name over and over each time you feed him or pick him up, and when you offer him a squeak toy or a special treat to eat. After a few days, stand several feet away from him and call him when you offer the treat or toy. Very soon he will learn to associate

A pair of ferrets looking intensely interested at a reward being offered.

"Like many animals, ferrets can be taught to come when called—and will do so most of the time."

"All of my ferrets invariably found exploring new territory to be spellbindingly fascinating, and they could do a very convincing 'deaf ferret' act when they were engaged in such activities, even when I went so far as to shout at them."

the sound of his name with your offering and you can gradually increase the distance from which you call him. It won't be long before he has learned that when you call his name, it means that there is something good in store for him—his dinner, a toy, a treat, or even just a play session—and he will usually be willing to come out from wherever he is to find out what you are up to.

Then again, there will also be times when your ferret won't come when you call him. These will most likely be instances in which your pet is exceptionally busy doing something which he finds more interesting than anything he thinks you might have to offer him at the time.

All of my ferrets invariably found exploring new territory to be spellbindingly fascinating, and they could do a very convincing "deaf ferret" act when they were engaged in such activities, even when I went so far as to shout at them.

Another time when your ferret may not come when you call him is when he is sleeping soundly. I found that often when my ferrets were snoozing, they were not willing to expend the energy to get up and come and see what I wanted—presumably because they were too comfortable and content to be bothered. Many times they would, however, at least momentarily wake up and lift their heads and look around before falling back to sleep. This would usually cause the bells on their collars to tinkle faintly once or twice—just enough to tell me where they were sleeping if I didn't already know.

SLEEP

On the other hand, ferrets are notoriously sound sleepers and, as many ferret owners can tell you from experience, these animals are perfectly capable of sleeping happily and snugly, curled up in some out of the way place without so much as twitching a whisker while you frantically scream out their name at the top of your lungs as you go from room to room trying to locate your lost pet—all the while certain that he must have gotten out the door when you weren't looking. These "lost" ferrets commonly turn up several hours later, nonchalantly yawning, refreshed from their nap and totally oblivious to all the worry and commotion that they have caused—and more often than not the location of their secret napping nook remains a mystery!

TRICKS

Ferrets are intelligent and fast learners and can easily be taught to do tricks. Even though I taught my skunk Eli to sit up on his hind legs and beg, it did not occur to me to try to teach the ferrets anything until I'd had McGuinn for a year and Melinda for a few weeks.

I started Melinda's lessons by saying the words "roll over" while I simultaneously grasped her by the shoulders and rolled her over. As soon as her feet hit the floor again I gave her a bite of raw beef kidney, which I find inedible but which she found to be very tasty. I repeated this procedure eight or nine times, and then I began to roll her over only three-quarters of the way. If she completed the roll she got a bite of kidney, and if she didn't we tried again. When she got to be fairly good at that I started rolling her over only half way—onto her back. If she completed the roll by going in the same direction in which I had started rolling her, she got her treat.

Ferrets are active, intelligent creatures that can be taught a number of tricks.

Keep in mind that all toys used in tricks must be safe. Sponge balls can be chewed into pieces and are therefore very dangerous.

After she had practiced that awhile I rolled her over a quarter of the way by gently pushing her over onto her side, all the while repeating the words "roll over" and rewarding her for her successes in doing so. Next I lightly brushed her shoulder as if I were starting to push her over onto her side and she would roll over on her own. Soon I had only to say "roll over" and wave my hand above her as if I were going to touch her shoulder, and she would eagerly roll over and look about expectantly for her bite of beef kidney.

All of this was accomplished in about three ten-minute lessons. It could not be done with only one session, simply because when she'd had her fill of beef kidney I could not keep her attention and she tended to wander off, putting an end to that particular lesson.

I was so pleased and encouraged by how quickly Melinda had learned to roll over that I immediately started lessons for McGuinn. She was willing to let me roll her over and would gladly eat her reward when I gave it to her, but when I tried to move on to the next step, she refused to cooperate and would invariably just get up and walk off. I attributed her disinterest and lack of cooperation to her age—I thought that perhaps because she was older she found such behavior foolish and undignified, whereas a young kit like Melinda might not mind acting silly. At any rate, when we were still on step one after 15 minutes of instruction, I finally decided that it was all a waste of time and I gave up the idea of trying to teach McGuinn anything.

In the meantime I discovered that Melinda was willing to roll over for almost anything edible—not just raw kidney. I was so proud of her that I filled my pockets with cat chow and for the next three days I had her performing her trick for friends,

The hard part about training ferrets involves getting and keeping their attention long enough for the desired behavior to be taught and carried out.

neighbors, and strangers on the street. All of this time McGuinn would just stand by and watch, trying to steal Melinda's reward whenever she could. On the fourth morning I was cooking bacon for breakfast and the ferrets were underfoot, as usual. I was totally astounded when I happened to glance down and see both Melinda and McGuinn rolling over. I took a bit of bacon and held it above McGuinn's head.

"Do you want some bacon, McGuinn? Roll over." To my amazement she immediately rolled over again, eagerly accepted the bacon, and then repeated the performance without any prompting. Both ferrets continued to roll over repeatedly until they'd had their fill of bacon. To this day I'm not sure when or how McGuinn learned to roll over. I think that it was most likely during the one lesson I gave her—when she learned what to do if she wanted to get the reward, but just hadn't wanted it badly enough

"To this day I'm not sure when or how McGuinn learned to roll over. I think it was most likely during the one lesson I gave her—when she learned what to do if she wanted to get the reward, but just hadn't wanted it badly enough. . . ."

". . .soon both ferrets had learned to use this action as a sort of language to ask for whatever they wanted."

Ferrets are clever creatures—clever enough to weigh the pros and cons before performing a new trick.

to be bothered with going to all the trouble and foolishness of rolling over! On the other hand, I can't say for certain that she didn't learn it from watching Melinda. Perhaps it was a combination of the two, but undeniably she did learn how to do it!

COMMUNICATION

For the next few weeks McGuinn remained reluctant to roll over, doing so only when she was highly motivated by the offer of a treat that she especially wanted. Melinda, silly kit that she was, continued to perform at the drop of a hat for just about anything—and sometimes for nothing at all! During the next month McGuinn gradually overcame her reluctance to roll over and soon both ferrets had learned to use this action as a sort of language to ask for whatever they wanted. They rolled over when they wanted food, a toy, to see something (such as what was in the paper bag or box), to be let out of their cage, to have a door opened for them, or to be picked up. Melinda would also roll over to get a kiss. They came to use this language to ask for such a wide variety of things that many times when they would walk up to me and roll over I would have absolutely no idea what they wanted!

Melinda and McGuinn were not unusual in their ability to use what they had been taught as a means of communication, however, as I know of numerous other ferrets that were taught a trick by their owners and quickly figured out that they could use the action to ask for whatever they wanted. Cindy Iglesias, a ferret owner in Baltimore, Maryland, wrote to tell me about her ferret, Slinky.

"It took us only three days to teach our Albino male, Slinky, to roll over. We discovered that he would do just about anything for watermelon, so we used little pieces of watermelon to teach him this trick. He soon discovered that he could roll over for other things he wanted and would roll for something to eat, to get into a room from which he was barred, and when he wanted

to get out off his cordoned-off room—and all of this without any prompting from us. Last summer when Slinky and our female Sable, came into season at the same time, we separated them because we did not want to breed Sable until she had been in heat for at least two weeks. One day after they had been apart for about ten days, I was carrying Sable around the apartment on my shoulder and I noticed that Slinky was following me wherever I went. He was getting under my feet, so I finally stopped and said to him, 'What on earth do you want, Slinky?' He looked up at me, then looked at Sable, and then rolled over about five times in a row. He wanted Sable!"

On occasion, Melinda, who always found her language successful in getting what she wanted from me, would carry it a step farther and would roll over to try to get what she wanted from an inanimate object. For example, one day while I was studying, I happened to glance into the next room and see Melinda trying to catch the toy I had suspended from a string for the ferret's entertainment. It was hanging five or six inches above her head so that she had to jump up at it, and on this particular day she just couldn't seem to catch it firmly between her teeth and it kept getting away from her. As usual, I found her

antics to be infinitely more entertaining than my physics book, so I sat at my desk and watched her through the open doorway for awhile without going into the room.

She must have leaped at the toy eight or ten times without catching it; it swung out of her reach every time. Finally, much to my amazement, she stopped and rolled over and then leaped at it again. When she failed to catch it she paused and looked up at it for awhile, rolled over a second time, and then leaped at it again. This time she was successful, and she caught it between her teeth and happily began chewing and tugging on it—trying to carry it away. I have never decided if she was especially smart to ask a toy to hold still and allow her to catch it, or just especially dumb. I suppose it all depends upon how you look at it. I prefer to think she was especially intelligent, as none of my other ferrets ever did it—at least not that I happened to see!

Melinda and McGuinn were both intelligent enough to learn very quickly that it was not safe to roll over while standing on a table or countertop. They had very good memories—it took them only one fall each, the result of rolling over too near the edge of the table, to impress them with the danger. They both refused to roll over on any

"... when Melinda and McGuinn were invited to do their tricks on the David Letterman show several years ago, I knew that if it was at all possible, it would be extremely difficult to get them to perform, and I was tempted to decline the invitation."

surface that was not level with the ground, no matter what the reward was or how badly they wanted it.

Melinda, however, who did not give up easily when she had her mind set on getting what she wanted, soon devised her own version of "roll over" which could safely be performed anywhere—at any level, both high and low. This consisted of turning around in a circle, a motion which I assume she found to be just as close as she could come to rolling over while still keeping all four feet securely planted on the ground.

It took almost a week of my saying "No, Melinda, roll over—not turn around," until I realized that she knew a new trick if I would only take advantage of it, and so I finally taught her the words "turn around" to go along with it. She immediately incorporated the new action into her repertoire, and when she wanted to ask for something she would first walk up to me and turn around. If what she wanted was not immediately forthcoming, then she would roll over. She always made her request by performing in that particular sequence—I think probably because turning around was easier and took less energy than rolling over, which she saved and used only if the easier action did not work to get her what she wanted. The only exception to this pattern was on those occasions when she was especially motivated by something she wanted more intensely than usual. At those times she was more aggressive and willing to expend more energy, and she would turn around and roll over repeatedly in rapid sequence, which seemed to serve as her method of adding "Oh, please!" to her request.

Ferrets aren't quite as eager to please as dogs are, and, consequently, mine would not usually do their tricks without a

good reason. Instead, they would only perform when they wanted something, either something they thought of on their own or something I would offer them. For the first several months Melinda would roll over on command, but she gradually gave this up and eventually would not roll over unless there was some type of reward involved. In addition, there were certain situations, such as when they were exploring a new environment, in which it was impossible to even get their attention, let alone get them to perform. At those times they were not in the least bit interested in anything I offered, no matter what it was, and I could depend on them to totally ignore me and go into their deaf ferret act when I asked them to roll over.

COMMAND PERFORMANCE

A television studio definitely falls within the realm of new territory, so when Melinda and McGuinn were invited to do their tricks on the David Letterman show several years ago, I knew that if it was at all possible, it would be extremely difficult to get them to perform, and I was tempted to decline the invitation. After giving the matter much thought and careful consideration and discussing it with the show's producer, I finally devised a plan which I thought might work and finally agreed, although with some reservations, to give it a try.

First I arranged to arrive at the studio more than three hours before the taping was to begin. When I got there and found it was to be a live broadcast, I became even more nervous about whether or not I could get my pets to perform—on live TV they would not get a second chance! I took Melinda and McGuinn into the empty studio and walked around for 15 minutes, letting them look at everything in the huge room.

Next, one of the stagehands set up the card table that was to serve as the "stage" upon which my pets were to perform. The producer had originally wanted me to let the ferrets down on the floor to do their tricks, but he agreed to let them perform on a table when I explained that it would be impossible to elicit their cooperation, not to mention even get their attention, once I put them down. From experience I knew that they would be so fully distracted by their desire to investigate the studio that they would most certainly and predictably just wander off, oblivious to my pleas of "roll over."

The table was placed in exactly the same location it was going to be in during the broadcast, and I put the

Ferrets' natural curiosity leads them to inspect almost everything they come across, including toys intended for other pets.

"From experience I knew that they would be so fully distracted by their desire to investigate the studio that they would most certainly and predictably just wander off, oblivious to my pleas of 'roll over.'"

A ferret looking intently, as if he's waiting for a reward.

"... since I had not fed them anything at all in the past 24 hours and had not given them anything to drink in the past ten hours ... hopefully they would be willing to do just about anything for a little drink of milk...."

ferrets on top of it and went away and left them there for the next two and a half hours. In doing this I hoped that they would look around at the interesting new territory long enough to transform it into "boring, old, we've-seen-this-before territory," giving me a better chance of getting their attention when the time came for me to tell them to roll over if they wanted a drink of milk.

Another thing I was counting on was that I was fairly certain that they were going to want a drink of milk. Under ordinary circumstances they were both crazy about milk, but since I had not fed them anything at

all in the past 24 hours and had not given them anything to drink in the past ten hours, I knew they were going to be especially hungry and thirsty, and hopefully they would be willing to do just about anything for a little drink of milk—including such a hazardous, risky thing as rolling over on top of a small table!

A few minutes before it was our turn to go on, I happened to run across the remains of a roast beef sandwich one of the stage crew had deserted at lunch. In a sudden fit of inspiration I took a piece of the beef and tore it into small bites, and when the time came and the cameras

were rolling, I was armed with food in addition to the milk to offer my poor hungry pets in exchange for their performance.

Both ferrets were so starved that the smell of beef and milk nearly drove them wild. I put them down on the table and immediately got their full and undivided attention when I asked if they wanted some milk. They totally ignored the now familiar room and the audience and tried to climb back up into my arms to get at the food. I backed away from the table out of their reach and repeated the question, holding the cup of milk up above their heads.

"Melinda, McGuinn, do you want some milk? Roll over." They both looked around the table for a few seconds, and then up at me. Melinda was the first to respond and, predictably, she turned around in a circle. "Now roll over, Melinda," I told her again. She turned around a second time and stood looking at me expectantly. "No, roll over," I repeated a third time, trying not to panic. "She's afraid she'll fall off the table if she rolls over," I explained to the audience.

Just at that very moment, when I was beginning to think that my plan had failed, Melinda's hunger and

". . . when the time came and the cameras were rolling, I was armed with food in addition to the milk to offer my poor hungry pets in exchange for their performance."

One ferret may be able to learn a given behavior by watching another perform the particular feat.

This ferret looks like he's about to take a well-deserved rest after a stimulating training session.

". . . I had thought that the David Letterman show was a local television show. It's probably a good thing I hadn't known—if I had I might not have been willing to take a chance on finding out whether or not I could get my little pets to roll over . . . on national TV!"

Opposite: Do not attempt to train your ferrets in an environment where there are distractions, i.e. outdoors or any new territory. In addition, train only one ferret at a time.

thirst finally overcame her fear and, much to my relief, she quickly rolled over. I rewarded her courage with a sip of milk and a bite of beef, which McGuinn promptly and unsuccessfully tried to steal. Melinda wanted more so she turned around and rolled over again, and at just about the same time McGuinn, too, finally got brave enough to roll over. I rewarded them and they both eagerly repeated the performance, which the audience loved!

Later that day, when I got home from the studio, I was surprised to find a message on my answering machine from Don and Marquita Robinson, ferret owners I know who live in Los Angeles. They had just called to say how much they had enjoyed seeing Melinda and McGuinn do their tricks on TV. I was shocked. Until I got their message I had thought that the David Letterman show was a local television show. It's probably a good thing I hadn't known—if I had I might not have been willing to take a chance on finding out whether or

not I could get my little pets to roll over on a tabletop in a new environment on national TV!

TRAINING AIDS

Later, in giving lessons to other ferrets, I experimented and found, quite reasonably, that they always learned much more quickly when I could get their full and undivided attention before I started to teach them anything. It soon became apparent that the most effective way to get their attention was to take away all their food after dinner at night, and then give them a lesson in the morning when they were hungry, using their breakfast as a reward.

Another thing I eventually discovered was that they also learned much faster with rapid, close-spaced repetition of whatever action I was trying to teach them—such as sit up, turn around, or roll over. I found that if I used milk rather than solid food as a reward, I could lower the

164

"Sometimes when I tried to teach older ferrets . . . they, like McGuinn, apparently didn't learn anything—only to show up later doing the trick when there was something they wanted."

Training ferrets can be fun and rewarding, but remember that you must have their complete attention during training sessions. If you don't, you probably won't get anywhere.

dish and let them have one or two laps, take it away, and have them perform again in a matter of seconds, whereas solid food took a longer time to eat and consequently increased the time span between each repetition. With milk I could put them through whatever action I was teaching them 50 or 60 times in five minutes, rather than only 15 or 20 times with solid foods. In such cases, most kits were able to learn the trick I was teaching them in just one five-minute lesson.

Sometimes when I tried to teach older ferrets using milk as a reward, they, like McGuinn, apparently didn't learn anything—only to show up later doing the trick when there was something they wanted.

Both Sally and her daughter Moseley, who were well over a year old when I finally got around to teaching them to roll over, each got only one five-minute session before I became impatient, lost interest, and abandoned the project, due to their lack of cooperation and apparent lack of progress. I did not give them their breakfast, however, and, much to my surprise, within about 15 minutes both of them, obviously hungry, came around to where I was studying and began to roll over!

MEMORY

Another thing I find impressive about ferrets, in addition to how quickly they are able to learn, is how well they are able to remember what they're taught. For example, several years ago I had a large litter of seven-week-old kits that I was selling. All of my pets at that time were females, so I decided to keep one of the White-footed males who seemed especially nice, and I separated him from the others in the litter. I took away his food that night after dinner and the next morning I taught him to roll over—which he learned in the usual five minutes.

The desire to gain the reward offered for successful completion of a trick will vary from individual to individual.

"Another thing I find impressive about ferrets . . . is how well they are able to remember what they're taught."

Before putting your ferret into his traveling crate, give him plenty of exercise so he will be more likely to settle down once you start your trip.

That afternoon a friend of mine came over and I got the ferret out and had him perform his new trick a few times. The following morning I decided that even though I didn't have any male ferrets, I already had too many pets, so I put him back in the cage to be sold with his littermates. Three weeks later someone came over to buy a ferret, and I mentioned that I had taught one of the White-footed males to roll over, but I couldn't tell them apart anymore and didn't know which one he was. I explained that he really never got any practice at this trick because I'd immediately put him back with the litter and never asked him to roll over again. Consequently, he probably wouldn't remember how but we could try anyway, just to see what would happen. I opened a can of cat food and held it above the cage and said, "Roll over." I must say I really was quite surprised when one of the White-footed kits rolled over without the least bit of hesitation. The potential buyer was just as

impressed as I was and she bought him on the spot!

The funniest thing that ever happened while I was giving lessons was with one little male Sable ferret, named Jack Hirschowitz, that I had sold as a kit and who came back to me to be put up for adoption when his owner moved out of the country and couldn't take him along. He was almost a year old, and I decided that it would make him more attractive to a new owner if I taught him a few tricks. As usual I gave him his first lesson early one morning when he was hungry. It didn't take him very long to figure out that I was only going to give him one little sip of milk at a time, and he wasn't at all happy with this arrangement, which he obviously thought was filling up his stomach far too slowly and with far too much effort. After getting his meager reward of only a taste of milk for four or five actions, he decided he'd had enough of that kind of nonsense and took the initiative to change the situation.

Ferrets have very good memories and may repeat a trick long after you thought they had never learned it.

"After getting his meager reward of only a taste of milk for four or five actions, he decided he'd had enough of that kind of nonsense and took the initiative to change the situation."

The author with two of the many ferrets she has known throughout the years.

"I was so impressed with how cleverly he had solved the problem I'd created for him that I just didn't have the heart to take his milk away. . . ."

The next time I lowered the bowl to the floor to let him have a sip of milk, instead of taking a drink as I expected, he very carefully picked up the dish between his teeth and carried it away in his mouth! I was so taken aback that I let him go, watching to see where he was going to take it.

Carrying it in front of him and spilling milk along the way, he headed straight for the refrigerator and tried to go behind it. When he discovered that he couldn't fit the dish in front of him, he turned around and backed into the narrow space tail first, and then he tried to pull the bowl in behind him. After struggling unsuccessfully for a minute or two to get his bowl of milk into a safe place (where I couldn't steal it away from him and hold it above his head again!), he finally gave up and started drinking it right where it was.

I was so impressed with how cleverly he had solved the problem I'd created for him that I just didn't have the heart to take his milk away from him, and consequently that put an end to his first lesson. It took a little longer to teach him all his tricks that way, but at least I didn't have to take his milk away from him anymore, which under the circumstances I just couldn't bring myself to do!

The ferret is a
fascinating
creature that
will provide its
owner with
entertainment
and
companionship
for many years.

Suggested Reading

All About Ferrets
By Mervin F. Roberts
ISBN 0-87666-914-3
TFH PS-754
Owner's manual for the care and management of a pet that is becoming increasingly popular throughout the world. Written by a well-known small mammal expert, *All About Ferrets* concentrates on the sensible, practical approach to making the addition and maintenance of a ferret easy on the animal and its owner alike. In addition, it gives plenty of helpful tips and a fine natural history background as well as beautiful photographic coverage.

Ferrets
By Wendy Winsted
ISBN 0-86622-829-2
TFH KW-074
Dr. Winsted's first T.F.H. ferret work, this hardcover book lets its readers know the best way to select and care for their pets. Easy to read and easy to learn from, it puts good advice in a form that even a novice can understand and profit from. Every topic of importance to a current and potential ferret owner is covered thoroughly, with attention put exactly where it belongs—on the basics.

Ferrets and Ferreting
By Graham Wellstead
ISBN 0-87666-938-0
TFH PS-792
Although not primarily concerning keeping ferrets as pets, this book will appeal to ferret owners who want to know how these animals are used to hunt small game—and it will appeal to the general hunting audience as well. Thoroughly enjoyable and full of stories on hunting and other ferret lore. Written for high school level and above.

A Step-by-Step Book About Ferrets
By Jay and Mary Field
Hardcover ISBN 0-86622-913-3
       TFH SK-009X
Softcover ISBN 0-86622-462-9
       TFH SK-009
A member of the step-by-step series, this little book will
appeal especially to beginners in the field of ferret keeping.
Full-color humorous drawings and illuminating photographs
enliven the practical, easy-to-read text.

Chinchilla Handbook
By Edmund Bickel
ISBN 0-86622-494-7
TFH PS-853
It is most likely that no one in the world had as much practical
experience with chinchillas as the author of this book, since he
began working with them in the early 1930s. His contributions
to the art and science of chinchilla management and breeding
are enormous, and all continental chinchilla owners owe him
a great debt for his pioneering work with these fascinating
animals. Finally, English-speaking chinchilla fanciers have a
chance to benefit from Edmund Bickel's vast experience as
well, as this book is a distillation of well over half a century of
his experiences with and observations of chinchillas from
every standpoint.

Chipmunks
By Chris Henwood
ISBN 0-86622-692-3
TFH KW-181
Hardy and easy to care for as well as being among the most
attractive of all small mammals, chipmunks have become
increasingly popular as pets. This book, written by one of the
world's foremost breeders/fanciers of chipmunks, is designed
to provide all the information that anyone would need in order
to keep chipmunks happy and healthy and to enjoy them to
their fullest. Illustrated throughout with full-color
photographs and drawings, the text is easy to read and put to
use.

Index

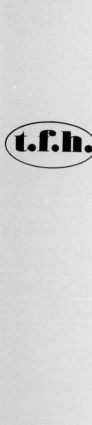

**FERRETS IN
YOUR HOME
TS-106**